THE

JESUS

HABITS

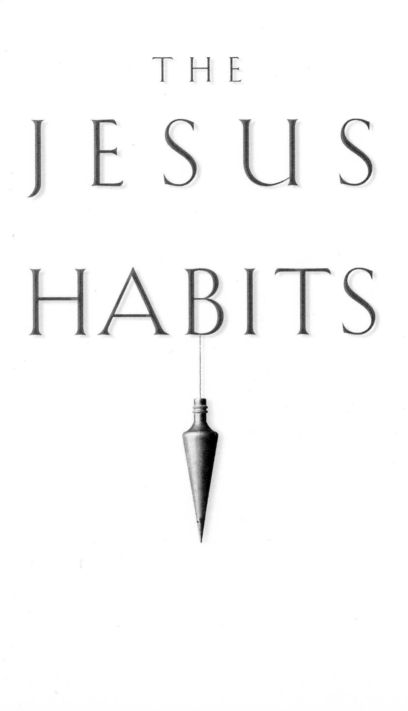

THE

JESUS

HABITS

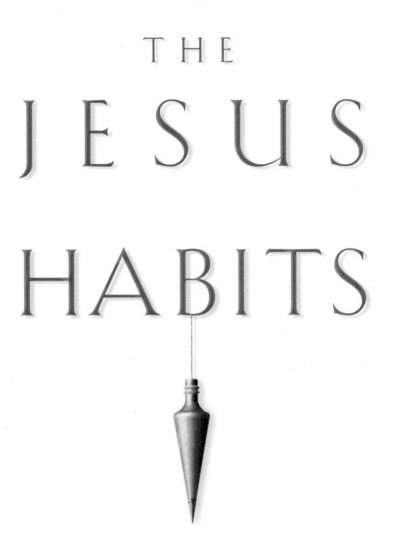

JAY DENNIS

BROADMAN
&HOLMAN
PUBLISHERS

0–8054–3127–6

Published by Broadman & Holman Publishers
Nashville, Tennessee

Unless otherwise noted, Scripture quotations are taken from the
New American Standard Bible, © the Lockman Foundation,
1960, 1962, 1963, 1968, 1971, 1972, 1973, 1975, 1977; used
by permission. Others quoted are marked KJV, King James
Version; MSG, *The Message,* Eugene H. Peterson, © 1993, 1994,
by Eugene H. Peterson, published by NavPress, Colorado
Springs, Colo.; NIV, The Holy Bible, New International Version,
copyright © 1973, 1978, 1984 by International Bible Society;
TLB, The Living Bible, copyright © Tyndale House Publishers,
Wheaton, Ill., 1971, used by permission.

Dewey Decimal Classification: 248.84
Subject Heading: CHRISTIAN LIFE \
JESUS CHRIST—HUMANITY

1 2 3 4 5 6 7 8 9 10 11 10 09 08 07 06 05

*I lovingly dedicate this book
to my precious wife and best friend, Angie,
and my two wonderful children, Will and Emily;
my great and supportive dad and mom,
Bill and Donna Dennis; and my father-in-law and
mother-in-law, E. W. and Millie Poe, who made possible
God's greatest gift to me outside of salvation.*

Each of these has made this life a little heaven on earth.

ACKNOWLEDGMENTS

How can one ever say thank you enough to the people who make writing a book like *The Jesus Habits* possible? My administrative assistant, Beth Miller, is a gift from God. Without her this work would have never survived the pressures of a busy pastor. Thank you, Beth, for thinking ahead of me and at times thinking for me.

To the great people of First Baptist Church at the Mall who love and encourage their pastor to pursue his passion to write, I say, "Thank you." You are the best congregation on earth.

Thank you, Howe Whitman and Neill Faucett, for believing in this project and encouraging me to go change the world for Christ.

Thank you, men who make up the Tuesday morning Bible study group, for allowing me to experiment with ideas that I have for Bible studies, including *The Jesus Habits*. John Prahl, thanks for helping me with this great group.

Thank you, men who gathered in my den one evening, for lovingly encouraging me, believing in my dreams, and offering godly counsel. Guys, I love you.

Thank you, Gwen Diaz and Karel Zelbovitz, for your incredible help in editing this book.

Thank you, Len Goss and John Landers of Broadman & Holman. These men are taking publishing to a new level.

Thank you, Lew Collier, who has become like family to me, and Rob Harper, who dreams with me of changing the world.

Thank you, Jimmy Draper, for being my pastor.

CONTENTS

INTRODUCTION
THE
JESUS HABITS

The world has always been fascinated with Jesus. Whether they receive him as Savior or not, the world is interested in this man Jesus, who he was and what he did. In 2004, Mel Gibson's movie *The Passion of the Christ* demonstrated this fascination. Over 45 percent of Americans either have seen the movie or plan to see it. It got the whole world talking about Jesus. One of the movie's directors said, "You can't spend 24–7 with Jesus and not be influenced." His life transcends all time, geographical, racial, social, and gender boundaries. Kenneth Scott Latourette said, "As the centuries pass, the evidence is accumulating that, measured by His effect on history, Jesus is the most influential life ever lived on this planet."

Napoleon Bonaparte said of Jesus:

> I know men; and I tell you that Jesus Christ is not a man. Superficial minds see a resemblance between Christ and the founders of empires, and the gods of other religions. That resemblance does not exist. There is between Christianity and whatever other religions, the distance of infinity. . . . Everything in Christ astonishes me. His spirit overawes me, and his will confounds me. Between him and whoever else in the world there is no possible term of comparison. He is truly a being by himself. His ideas and his sentiments, the truth which he announces, his manner of convincing, are not explained either by human organization or by the nature of things. . . . I search in vain in history to find the

similar to Jesus Christ, or anything which can approach
the gospel.[1]

The Jesus Habits—thirty-one of them—are observable patterns
in the life of Jesus Christ. He is the consummate example for successful living. The good news for you and me is that each of these
habits can be copied; they can be put to practice in our daily lives.
Many leaders throughout the centuries have been held up as worthy of emulating, but no one in history is more worthy of imita-
tion than Jesus Christ. Jesus said, "For I gave you an example that
you also should do as I did to you" (John 13:15). He further gave
us the key to happiness, and it comes back to doing what he did.
"If you know these things, you are blessed if you do them" (John
13:17). *Blessed* means "to be happy." Happiness comes through a
set of habits, *The Jesus Habits*.

The idea for this book began when the Lord placed upon my
heart to begin reading the Gospels and observe what Jesus did,
not just what he taught. Now to be sure, everything he taught he
practiced. But as I started making notes in my wide-margin Bible,
I went back and noticed how many times I had written the word
habit beside something Jesus did. Looking back, I found thirty-one
identifiable habits of Jesus. William Paley said, "A large part of
Christian virtue consists in right habits." When we hear the word
habit, we generally think of something negative, something that
could hurt us. But habits can be good. In *The Jesus Habits* I am asking you to exchange a bad habit for a Jesus habit. With his
strength, you can. John Dryden said, "We first make our habits,
then our habits make us." Dr. Michael Mitchell, author of *Building
Strong Families,* said, "Approximately 90 percent of what we do
every day is governed by the habits in our lives." A Princeton
University study claims if you do the same thing every day for
twenty-eight consecutive days it will become a habit.[2]

I am your constant companion; I am your greatest
helper or heaviest burden. I will push you onward or
drag you down to failure. I am completely at your command. Half the things you do, you might just as well
turn over to me, and I will be able to do them quickly

and correctly. I am easily managed—you must merely be firm with me. Show me exactly how you want something done, and after a few lessons I will do it automatically. I am the servant of all great people and, alas, of all failures as well. Those who are great, I have made great. Those who are failures, I have made failures. I am not a machine, though I work with all the precisions of a machine plus the intelligence of a human. You may run me for profit or run me for ruin—it makes no difference to me. Take me, train me, be firm with me, and I will place the world at your feet. Be easy with me, and I will destroy you. Who am I? I am Habit.[3]

Pollster George Barna, in his book, *Think Like Jesus,* says, "Consider the range of the benefits emerging from thinking and living like Jesus. We are promised physical gain, emotional benefits, superior decision-making capacity, relational advantages, lifestyle enhancements, and spiritual health. The more we devote ourselves to emulating the thought and behavioral patterns of Jesus, the more God is able to bless us and use us for His purposes."[4]

The thirty-one Jesus habits will lead to your greatest days of blessing and success. You will discover that some passages are used more than once because of their multiple applications.

I want you to consider three things as you read this book:

1. The Jesus habits can become your habits, too.
2. You have to be willing to do whatever it takes to make each habit a part of your life.
3. Through Jesus Christ you have the power to stop a bad habit and begin a Jesus habit. You have prayer, the Holy Spirit, the Bible, faith, and godly people to assure your success.

Now let's begin a journey—the most exciting journey of your life—of exercising the spiritual disciplines of Jesus.

THE HABIT OF
SECLUSION

POINT PASSAGE

*In the early morning, while it was still dark, Jesus got up,
left the house, and went away to a secluded place,
and was praying there.*

MARK 1:35

The Jesus habit of seclusion is withdrawing, momentarily or for an extended period of time, from everyday noise and demands, to spend some time with God for the purpose of connecting with God and allowing your emotional and spiritual batteries to be recharged. This is time built into your daily schedule, no matter how busy and complicated that schedule might be. Yet in our society, finding a place of seclusion is becoming increasingly difficult.

> The word *seclusion* means "an act of setting somebody or something apart from others. A quiet place removed from activity and people."

Jesus Showed Us the Habit of Seclusion

Jesus got tired, hungry, weary, sleepy, exhausted.
He yawned.

His eyes got red and bloodshot.

His feet hurt.

His mind got weary.

Everywhere Jesus went he was confronted with crowds, demands, noise, requests, opinions, advice, criticisms, and interruptions.

He continually heard:
"Heal me!"
   "Touch me!"
      "Help me!"
         "Do something!"
            "Intervene!"
               "I need a miracle!"
                  "Solve this!"
                     "Come here!"
                        "Go there!"
"Prove it!"
   "Stop it!"
      "Do it!"

You Have Ear Worms

Ear worms? I couldn't believe what I was hearing on a radio interview. The host announced, "We have all had ear worms." Immediately I felt my right ear starting to itch. But didn't I get inoculated for that when I was a kid? Maybe not.

Ear worms are songs you have heard that you can't get out of your mind. In an article "'Earworms' Bother Women, Musicians Most," we learn: "They bore into your head. They won't let go. There's no known cure. Earworms can attack almost anyone at almost any time. No it's not an invasion of jungle insects. It's worse. Earworms are those songs, jingles, and tunes that get stuck inside your head."

As you rewind in your mind, think about those songs that have stuck—songs like "YMCA,"

"Who Let the Dogs Out," "Whoomp—There It Is," "Mamas Don't Let Your Babies Grow Up to Be Cowboys," "Dancing Queen," or the Kit Kat candy bar jingle, "Gimme a Break." Each of us has our own ear worms.

The only cure for ear worms, and the noise with which we are daily bombarded, is a time of quiet seclusion. As I am writing this chapter, my doctor has me on a weeklong fast from talking due to a vocal condition. He and my wife knew that in order for me to do that I must get away from home and church and be secluded. I fussed initially, but as I sit on the balcony of a friend's condo overlooking the Gulf of Mexico, I can feel myself reenergizing through my disconnection.[1]

> "Show me!"
>
> "Listen to me!"
>
> "Give me!"

These constant demands drain the body, deplete the emotions, sap the spirit, and stress the soul. That's why we see Jesus— between those demands—going off by himself because he needed to be renewed, restored, and recharged.

Jesus often took time to withdraw from people, pressures, and the daily noises of life. Although he was not a loner, he did feel a need to be alone to refresh himself spiritually and emotionally. As fully human, as much as being fully God, he needed to recharge his spiritual and emotional batteries. If the Son of God needed seclusion, how much more do we need it? What happens in seclusion determines, for the most part, what happens publicly. Look back and ask yourself, "When did God speak to me most clearly?" I would venture to say that it was during those times when you and God were alone.

When Jesus withdrew, he often preferred two places: around the water and the mountains.

> After He had sent the crowds away, He went up on the mountain by Himself to pray; and when it was evening, He was there alone. (Matt. 14:23)
>
> Now when Jesus heard about John, He withdrew from there in a boat to a secluded place by Himself; and when the people heard of this, they followed Him on foot from the cities. (Matt. 14:13)
>
> So Jesus, perceiving that they were intending to come and take Him by force to make Him king, withdrew again to the mountain by Himself alone. (John 6:15)

The seaside and the mountains are both excellent settings to experience God. However, these places may have to be reserved for those times you can get away. It isn't probable that you could have that kind of setting everyday. Water speaks of life, even the storms of life, yet spending time with God can overcome those storms. Mountains speak of strength beyond. Spending time with God gives you strength to deal with anything that comes your way.

Why Jesus, as a Habit, Went into Seclusion
To hear God the Father more clearly

Then Jesus came with them to a place called Gethsemane, and said to His disciples, "Sit here while I go over there and pray." And He took with Him Peter and the two sons of Zebedee, and began to be grieved and distressed. Then He said to them, "My soul is deeply grieved, to the point of death; remain here and keep watch with Me."

And He went a little beyond them, and fell on His face and prayed, saying, "My Father, if it is possible, let this cup pass from Me; yet not as I will, but as You will." And He came to the disciples and found them sleeping, and said to Peter, "So, you men could not keep watch with Me for one hour? Keep watching and praying that you may not enter into temptation; the spirit is willing, but the flesh is weak."

He went away again a second time and prayed, saying, "My Father, if this cannot pass away unless I drink it, Your will be done." Again He came and found them sleeping, for their eyes were heavy. And He left them again, and went away and prayed a third time, saying the same thing once more. Then He came to the disciples and said to them, "Are you still sleeping and resting? Behold, the hour is at hand and the Son of Man is being betrayed into the hands of sinners. Get up, let us be going; behold, the one who betrays Me is at hand!" (Matt. 26:36–46)

In the garden of Gethsemane, Jesus withdrew so he could more clearly understand the will of the Father. There are times when the noise of the world makes our options too muffled and unclear. With what seems like everyone offering opinions, it's easy to listen to wrong advice. This is a time-out that says, "God, what is it you want me to do?" As Jesus demonstrates, it is not always convenient, but it is necessary and will bring about a clarity concerning God's will.

To pray

>   After He had sent the crowds away, He went up on
> the mountain by Himself to pray; and when it was
> evening, He was there alone. (Matt. 14:23)

>   But Jesus Himself would often slip away to the
> wilderness and pray. (Luke 5:16)

QUIET TIME WITHOUT NAP MATS

"One hour of quiet concentration in any business can be worth two hours of normal working time, according to the management of a Denver business, quoted in a Success magazine item.

"Interruptions are the biggest enemy of creativity," says Gary Desmond, a principal of Hoover Berg Desmond (HBD), a $30 million a year architectural firm. To minimize the inevitable interruptions in the firm's large, open offices, Desmond came up with the idea, which is more familiar to kids than corporations—the quiet hour. Every morning from 10 a.m. to 11 a.m., no one at HBD, including the principals, may communicate with anyone else inside or outside the office. "Basically, we're sitting at our desks for that hour," says Desmond, who makes allowances for emergency phone calls. "We try to focus totally on our clients' designs." Initially, HBD's 25 employees balked at the concept. "Management had to explain that this was not a response to bad work habits. It was a vehicle to make us concentrate even more rigorously," says Desmond, although he now concedes that quiet hour is an excellent crack-the-whip technique, too. But what do the clients think of it? At first, the firm chose to hide the policy from the outside world. "Businesses that found out used to ask if we served milk and cookies at quiet hour," says Desmond. "But we stuck to it and now those same firms respect how much we're trying to accomplish every morning." Quiet hour has worked out so well, in fact, that HBD wants to start a second one, perhaps in mid-afternoon. "Our employees all wish they had more quiet hours," says Desmond. "It gives us what most businesses need so badly, a little time to think."[2]

Jesus had to get away to pray. People simply wouldn't leave him alone long enough for him to communicate with the Father. His withdrawal demonstrated the priority of prayer in his life, not just for the sake of praying but for intimate time with the Father.

To recharge spiritually and emotionally

Now when Jesus heard about John, He withdrew from there in a boat to a secluded place by Himself; and when the people heard of this, they followed Him on foot from the cities. (Matt. 14:13)

And He healed many who were ill with various diseases, and cast out many demons; and He was not permitting the demons to speak, because they knew who He was. In the early morning, while it was still dark, Jesus got up, left the house, and went away to a secluded place, and was praying there. (Mark 1:34–35)

> The great danger is not that we will renounce our faith. It is that we will become so rushed and preoccupied that we will settle for a mediocre version of it.
> —John Ortberg

Jesus had just received news about his friend and forerunner, John the Baptist, being beheaded. When we receive bad news, it depletes us emotionally and can sap us spiritually. Further, the demands of performing miracles, healing people, and doing ministry drained him. He used his time alone with God to get refreshed. We are more vulnerable to temptation during times of spiritual and emotional emptiness.

To eat

And He said to them, "Come away by yourselves to a secluded place and rest a while." (For there were many people coming and going, and they did not even have time to eat.) They went away in the boat to a secluded place by themselves. (Mark 6:31–32)

Jesus and the disciples had become too busy to eat. Eating is vital to keep up your physical strength. But there can be added benefits. Some of your best times with God can be while eating alone. This is not to suggest becoming antisocial; it is, however, a time when you can reflect, think, pray, and eat.

To gain the right perspective

> So Jesus, perceiving that they were intending to come
> and take Him by force to make Him king, withdrew again
> to the mountain by Himself alone. (John 6:15)

The crowds wanted an earthly, reigning, military Messiah. When they were attempting to force him, Jesus withdrew in order to get the right perspective. It's important to back off, take a breath, and get God's perspective.

To learn to do spiritual battle

> Then Jesus was led up by the Spirit into the wilder-
> ness to be tempted by the devil. And after He had fasted
> forty days and forty nights, He then became hungry.
> And the tempter came and said to Him, "If You are the
> Son of God, command that these stones become bread."
> But He answered and said, "It is written, 'Man shall not
> live on bread alone, but on every word that proceeds
> out of the mouth of God.'"
>
> Then the devil took Him into the holy city and had
> Him stand on the pinnacle of the temple, and said to
> Him, "If You are the Son of God, throw Yourself down;
> for it is written, 'He will command His angels concern-
> ing You'; and 'On their hands they will bear You up, so
> that You will not strike Your foot against a stone.'" Jesus
> said to him, "On the other hand, it is written, 'You shall
> not put the Lord Your God to the test.'"
>
> Again, the devil took Him to a very high mountain
> and showed Him all the kingdoms of the world and their
> glory; and he said to Him, "All these things I will give
> You, if You fall down and worship me." Then Jesus said
> to him, "Go, Satan! For it is written, 'You shall worship
> the Lord your God, and serve Him only.'" Then the

devil left Him; and behold, angels came and began to minister to Him. (Matt. 4:1–11)

Jesus learned to do spiritual battle during those times of seclusion. Satan attacked him with everything he had, yet Jesus learned privately how to deal with public enemy number one—Satan. Our greatest attacks spiritually come, and our greatest victories are won, most often during those times of seclusion.

To listen to God

Jesus' times of seclusion were planned so that he could listen to God. Our quiet times must not be controlled by our telling God something, our talking to God, but in listening to him.

What Are the Enemies of the Habit of Seclusion?

1. Guilt—I will feel guilty for stopping what I'm doing just for a few minutes of being alone.
2. Busyness—I just don't have the time.
3. Ego—I can't afford to be away from what's going on. I'm needed.
4. Boredom—I will get too bored.
5. Uneasiness—I won't know what to say, what to do.
6. Awkwardness—Silence makes me feel weird.
7. People—What will others think?

We often face the enemies of busyness or hurry-sickness when we get overloaded, overcommitted, and overextended. Instituting the Jesus habit of seclusion is an antidote for our maladies caused by hurry and noise.

Make Seclusion a Habit

1. Give yourself permission to have a time of seclusion, a daily spiritual retreat with God.

Come to the place where you realize that not coming apart in seclusion could mean you will come apart in exhaustion, both spiritually and emotionally. Some feel guilty for taking time to back off even for a few minutes. Keep practicing seclusion, however, and you will notice the guilt is replaced with an anticipation for these times.

FOUR HELPS TO THE HABIT OF SECLUSION

1. Meditation

Biblical meditation involves emptying the mind and filling it with God's Word. It is tuning out the world and tuning into a specific Scripture or attribute of God. Choose to block out everything else for a specific period of time. Focus upon Jesus and the words of the Bible.

"This book of the law shall not depart from your mouth, but you shall meditate on it day and night, so that you may be careful to do according to all that is written in it; for then you will make your way prosperous, and then you will have success" (Josh. 1:8).

2. Disconnection

A time comes each day when we need to disconnect from the computer, the telephone, cell phones, pagers, VCRs, DVDs, TVs, and radios. In other words, disengaging from anything that beeps, blows, goes off, rings, honks, or says, "You've got mail." In sports it would be called a time-out.

3. Concentration

We need times of being still and simply listening to God. Too often we are moving targets,

moving too quickly to hear what God has to say to us. Concentration is a way to practice silence before God. We deliberately think about God.

4. Relaxation

Seclusion allows us to relax, to catch our breath, and to push pause for a moment. Seclusion does not mean isolation from the world. It is, however, a momentary "push-pause" for the purpose of recharging the human batteries. Jesus never withdrew permanently from the world, refusing to engage the culture in order to transform it. All you need is a place of seclusion where there are no interruptions, no noise, and no one else around. It can be as near as closing a door in a room, a quiet walk, a drive out of town, or underneath a tree. Get creative in finding those places. We need daily times of solitude, and we need times of extended solitude every month or two. Whether daily or extended, these must be scheduled and placed as priorities on your calendar. I cannot describe the sense of peace and connection with God due to a deliberate choice to have a time of seclusion.

2. Choose a specific time and place.

Calendar it. You need to know that there will be a set-aside place and time where you deliberately call a time-out. If you don't calendar it, the urgent will take the place of the necessary.

3. When the need arises, don't wait; do it immediately!

Sometimes we can't wait for a scheduled time-out. Something happens, someone says something, you feel things closing in on you, and the pressure is mounting. It's "excuse me" time. Just take a few minutes to regain your bearings by pulling away.

4. Be honest about what you are doing.

Let people know up front, "I need some time to think and pray." There is power in honesty. People may not understand it, but when you say, "I need to pray about this," or "I need a little time to think this through," they can respect it. Make sure, however, that it's not just a cop-out or a stalling technique.

5. Experiment with different places.

Try different rooms, go outside, drive somewhere peaceful, take a walk. You will discover that different places meet different needs.

6. Don't compromise by having a cell phone, handheld computer, or radio.

Seclusion is not possible if you are concerned about checking an e-mail or answering your cell phone. Life will go on without you for a few minutes. It will be hard at first, but you will grow to love these quiet moments.

7. Have a specific passage of Scripture that you want to think about.

Have a plan where you know what passage of Scripture you will use to allow God to speak to you. The flop-and-stop method (where you flop open the Bible and wherever it stops, that is what you read) isn't a good plan. The One-Year Bible is a great tool.

8. Take your Bible, a notebook, and a pen.

Write down insights, thoughts, and ideas God gives to you. Always have a copy of the Bible handy. Be a note taker. Journal the insights God gives to you. You will often forget them if not. You will get great encouragement as you look back on how God spoke to you. Further, it has a therapeutic effect when you write down your thoughts.

9. Be silent. Get still. Listen.

Practice being still. You might call it a holy "shut up." Encountering God centers around our listening to God. In our hurry-up world, it will take discipline to learn to be still.

10. Tell God you will be back at the same time tomorrow.

Promise him. Anticipate your time with God. If you are worried, concerned, frustrated, or fretting, put it in the "seclusion time" file and then confront it.

THE HABIT OF
PRAYER

POINT PASSAGE

*It happened that while Jesus was praying in a certain place,
after He had finished, one of His disciples said to Him, "Lord,
teach us to pray just as John also taught his disciples."*
LUKE 11:1

The Jesus habit of prayer is choosing to live in an atmosphere, either at a set time, or spontaneously—as a way of life—where you . . .

- Praise God.
- Thank God.
- Confess your sin to God.
- Ask on behalf of other people.
- Present your personal requests to God.

> The moment you wake up each morning, all your wishes and hopes for the day rush at you like wild animals. And the first job each morning consists in shoving it all back; in listening to that other voice, taking that other point of view, letting that other, larger, stronger, quieter life come flowing in.
> —C. S. Lewis

Jesus Showed Us How to Pray

The disciples were eavesdropping on Jesus while he was praying. They were so moved by what they heard they requested he teach them how to pray like he prayed. That's the key, learning to pray like Jesus prayed. They saw Jesus' power, and they connected the dots back to prayer.

When Jesus prayed

We gain insight into the times Jesus prayed and the significance these have in our own lives.

He prayed early in the morning.

In the early morning, while it was still dark, Jesus got up, left the house, and went away to a secluded place, and was praying there. (Mark 1:35)

Why is it important to pray then?

1. To prepare for the day.
2. To get ready for spiritual battle.

He prayed at night, sometimes all night.

It was at this time that He went off to the mountain to pray, and He spent the whole night in prayer to God. (Luke 6:12)

PRAYER AND THE DC SNIPER

Fifty Christian truckers got together to pray that somehow the sniper terrorizing the Washington, DC area would be caught. The snipers killed ten and wounded three around our nation's capital. Ron Lantz would be retiring as a driver in a few days and didn't even live in the area, but he felt sure that God would answer their prayers. A few days later he was listening to the radio as he was driving again through the region and felt compelled to pull off the highway to a rest stop. It was just a couple of miles from where the prayer meeting had taken place. As he pulled in, he was shocked to see a car similar to what was being described on the radio right there before his eyes. Carefully trying to read the license plate, a chill went up his back as the numbers matched. He quickly called 911 and remained there for what he said were the longest fifteen minutes of his life until the police arrived. He even pulled his truck across the exit. There would now be no escape for these elusive murderers. The rest is now history. The snipers were taken into custody without incident. Ron's testimony is being beamed around the world today. It shows the power of prayer. And in a class act, showing his true character, when asked what he would do with the award money, he said the half million dollars would simply be given to the victims' families.[1]

There are times when praying is more important than sleeping.

How Jesus prayed

He prayed with people and not just for them.

Some eight days after these sayings, He took along Peter and John and James, and went up on the mountain to pray. (Luke 9:28)

Take time to pray with your family and friends. If you promise to pray, immediately pray or write it down and pray later.

He prayed continually.

He never gave up in prayer.

Now He was telling them a parable to show that at all times they ought to pray and not to lose heart. (Luke 18:1)

Jesus prayed

- Looking up.

Jesus spoke these things; and lifting up His eyes to heaven, He said, "Father, the hour has come; glorify Your Son, that the Son may glorify You." (John 17:1)

- Kneeling.

And He withdrew from them about a stone's throw, and He knelt down and began to pray. (Luke 22:41)

- Falling on his face.

And He went a little beyond them, and fell on His face and prayed, saying, "My Father, if it is possible, let this cup pass from Me; yet not as I will, but as You will." (Matt. 26:39)

- Before making major decisions.

It was at this time that He went off to the mountain to pray, and He spent the whole night in prayer to God. (Luke 6:12)

- After great victories.

After He had sent the crowds away, He went up on the mountain by Himself to pray; and when it was evening, He was there alone. (Matt. 14:23)

• To overcome temptation.

And He came out and proceeded as was His custom to the Mount of Olives; and the disciples also followed Him. When He arrived at the place, He said to them, "Pray that you may not enter into temptation." And He withdrew from them about a stone's throw, and He knelt down and began to pray. (Luke 22:39–41)

> Oh! It's a glorious fact, that prayers are noticed in heaven.
> —C. H. Spurgeon

• Praising God the Father.

Jesus spoke these things; and lifting up His eyes to heaven, He said, "Father, the hour has come; glorify Your Son, that the Son may glorify You." (John 17:1)

• With a right motive.

"This is eternal life, that they may know You, the only true God, and Jesus Christ whom You have sent." (John 17:3)

• For intimacy with God.

"Now, Father, glorify Me together with Yourself, with the glory which I had with You before the world was." (John 17:5)

• Holding nothing back.

"While I was with them, I was keeping them in Your name which You have given Me; and I guarded them and not one of them perished but the son of perdition, so that the Scripture would be fulfilled." (John 17:12)

• A hedge of protection around his disciples.

"I do not ask You to take them out of the world, but to keep them from the evil one." (John 17:15)

• Based on Scripture.

"Sanctify them in the truth; Your word is truth." (John 17:17)

• To impact the world.

"I do not ask You to take them out of the world, but to keep them from the evil one." (John 17:15)

- During a crisis.

When the sixth hour came, darkness fell over the whole land until the ninth hour. At the ninth hour Jesus cried out with a loud voice, "Eloi, Eloi, lama sabachthani?" which is translated, "My God, My God, why have You forsaken Me?" (Mark 15:33–34)

- Fervently, passionately.

And being in agony He was praying very fervently; and His sweat became like drops of blood, falling down upon the ground. (Luke 22:44)

- While dying.

About the ninth hour Jesus cried out with a loud voice, saying, "Eli, Eli, lama sabachthani?" that is, "My God, My God, Why have You forsaken Me?" . . . And Jesus cried out again with a loud voice, and yielded up His spirit. (Matt. 27:46, 50)

What Are the Enemies of the Habit of Prayer?
1. Praying for the wrong reasons

You ask and do not receive, because you ask with wrong motives, so that you may spend it on your pleasures. (James 4:3)

2. Praying while hanging onto sin

If I regard wickedness in my heart,
the Lord will not hear. (Ps. 66:18)

3. Praying when you have had a closed Bible

He who turns away his ear from listening to the law,
Even his prayer is an abomination. (Prov. 28:9)

When you are indifferent to God's Word, neglect God's Word, or avoid God's Word, it will shut up heaven.

4. Praying but not believing God will answer

But he must ask in faith without any doubting, for the one who doubts is like the surf of the sea, driven and tossed by the wind. For that man ought not to expect that he will receive anything from the Lord. (James 1:6–7)

5. Praying with God not being number one

"Son of man, these men have set up their idols in their hearts and have put right before their faces the stumbling block of their iniquity. Should I be consulted by them at all?" (Ezek. 14:3)

6. Praying with hypocrisy

"When you pray, you are not to be like the hypocrites; for they love to stand and pray in the synagogues and on the street corners so that they may be seen by men. Truly I say to you, they have their reward in full." (Matt. 6:5)

7. Praying with an unforgiving spirit

"Whenever you stand praying, forgive, if you have anything against anyone so that your Father also who is in heaven may forgive you your transgressions." (Mark 11:25)

"Therefore if you are presenting your offering at the altar, and there remember that your brother has something against you, leave your offering there before the altar and go; first be reconciled to your brother, and then come and present your offering. Make friends quickly with your opponent at law while you are with him on the way, so that your opponent may not hand you over to the judge, and the judge to the officer, and you be thrown into prison. Truly I say to you, you will not come out of there until you have paid up the last cent." (Matt. 5:23–26)

8. Praying while there is conflict in your marriage

In the same way, you wives, be submissive to your own husbands so that even if any of them are disobedient to the word, they may be won without a word by the behavior of their wives, as they observe your chaste and respectful behavior. Your adornment must not be merely external—braiding the hair, and wearing gold jewelry, or putting on dresses; but let it be the hidden person of the heart, with the imperishable quality of a gentle and quiet spirit, which is precious in the sight of God. For in this way in former times the holy women also, who hoped in God, used to adorn themselves, being submissive to their own husbands; just as Sarah obeyed Abraham, calling him lord, and you have become her children if you do what is right without being frightened by any fear.

You husbands in the same way, live with your wives in an understanding way, as with someone weaker, since she is a woman; and show her honor as a fellow heir of the grace of life, so that your prayers will not be hindered. (1 Pet. 3:1–7)

9. Praying without being a Christian

Remember that you were at that time separate from Christ, excluded from the commonwealth of Israel, and strangers to the covenants of promise, having no hope and without God in the world. (Eph. 2:12 TLB)

10. Prayers that never get offered

"You do not have because you do not ask." (James 4:2)

Make Prayer a Habit

1. Choose to pray; don't wait until you feel like it.

Prayer is not about waiting for a right feeling; it is a habit, a choice, something you do regardless of how you feel. Prayer is a discipline of doing, not a matter of feeling.

2. Make prayer a part of your day, not just a set time.

You can pray at any place and at any time. Some people call these "arrow prayers"; you shoot them up immediately upon a need entering your life. You don't even have to close your eyes and get on your knees.

3. Pray Scripture back to God.

Take a passage of Scripture and pray it back to God. Take the promises of God and pray them back to God—applying them to you. Scriptural praying is the most powerful form of praying. Knowing that God honors his Word, there is a great confidence as we pray the Scriptures back to him.

4. Decide never to make a major decision without praying about it first.

To decide without getting God's opinion can bring all manner of problems that could have been avoided. Give God the opportunity to meet your need before taking matters into your own hands.

5. Pray before leaving your home in the morning.

Say a prayer before you leave in the morning. Pray for and about your day. Commit it to God. Ask for his blessing, protection, divine insight, and divine appointments.

6. Confess sin immediately.

Once you are aware you have sinned, stop what you are doing and immediately confess it. Get it right with God. Unconfessed sin will affect every area of your life and hinder God's great plan for you.

7. Try different positions for prayer—standing, sitting, kneeling, on your face.

Experiment, but remember it's the condition of the heart not the position of the body that God is observing. However, the position of your body can be an indicator of your heart. For instance, kneeling is an indication of one's submission to God.

8. Keep it simple.

Concentrate on being real before God, not worrying about the words you say. Prayer is a conversation with God. He is not impressed with our tone of voice or volume. Just talk to God in your own way.

9. Never give up. Keep on praying.

God has promised to bless our persistency. Since prayer must be grounded in faith, it becomes a testing time for the seriousness of our faith.

10. Expect answers.

Faith is expectation. Expect that God will answer your prayer. He will answer your prayers in one of four ways—"Yes," "No," "Wait," or "I've got something else, something better."

THE HABIT OF
WORSHIP

*"For where two or three have gathered together in My name,
I am there in their midst."*
MATTHEW 18:20

The Jesus habit of worship is an expression, an encounter, and an experience with God. It is an encounter that is initiated by your focusing on him and

> Christian worship is the most momentous, the most urgent, the most glorious action that can take place in human life.
> —Karl Barth

- Praising him for who he is.
- Thanking him for what he has done.
- Confessing your sin.
- Surrendering your mind, will, and emotions.
- Offering him your total life.
- Obeying what he tells you to do.
- Asking him to work in your life.
- Telling others of your love for him.
- Experiencing new love for him and a new commitment to him.

Jesus Showed Us about Worship

Jesus consistently worshipped God the Father. He made a habit to be in God's house—the place where he would most likely experience God. Jesus showed us that worship is personal, yet it is also corporate—coming together with other believers. He showed us that God's house is a house of prayer, a house of hearing God's Word, and a house of healing, where we worship God, focusing on inwardly worshipping him based on Scripture.

Worship, however, is not limited to church. Private worship prepares us for corporate worship. Going to church is safe. Let me prove it. A friend of mine sent me an article that suggested:

- 20 percent of all fatal accidents occur while riding in automobiles.
- 17 percent of all accidents occur in the home.
- 11 percent of accidents occur to pedestrians while walking on streets or sidewalks.
- 16 percent of all accidents take place through air, rail, or water travel.
- Of the remaining 33 percent, 32 percent of deaths occur in hospitals.

Now here is the good news. Only .001 percent of all deaths occur in worship services in church. Therefore, one of the safest places on earth is in a worship service. I suppose we could start a bumper sticker that states, "GOING TO CHURCH CAN SAVE YOUR LIFE."

Jesus was consistent in worship.

> At that time Jesus said to the crowds, "Have you come out with swords and clubs to arrest Me as you would against a robber? Every day I used to sit in

---

WEBSTER ON WORSHIP

There is a great lesson to be learned from the dictionary. When things start going bad, we often fear they will only get worse. It seems that "worse" will take us to the "worst." To prevent the "worse" from turning into the "worst," look at the unique set-up God has provided in the English language. Any standard dictionary will separate the words *worse* (and its derivatives) and *worst* with one special word—*worship*. When circumstances seem to be slipping in the wrong direction, remember that worship is the buffer between *worse* and *worst*.

—Darrin Ethier[1]

the temple teaching and you did not seize Me." (Matt. 26:55)

Every day Jesus would go to the temple, showing his consistency and the priority of corporate worship. Worship should be a way of life, not limited to a particular day of the week.

Jesus had a passion about God's house.

His disciples remembered that it was written, "Zeal for Your house will consume me." (John 2:17)

The word *zeal* means "passion, fervor, enthusiasm." Jesus was passionate about God's house because it was a place through which people could encounter God.

Jesus demonstrated that having children in God's house must become a priority.

But when the chief priests and the scribes saw the wonderful things that He had done, and the children who were shouting in the temple, "Hosanna to the Son of David," they became indignant and said to Him, "Do You hear what these children are saying?" And Jesus said to them, "Yes; have you never read, 'Out of the mouth of infants and nursing babies you have prepared praise for yourself'?" (Matt. 21:15–16)

Having children in church helps to set their moral and spiritual compass. Jesus wants children in church.

Jesus understood that people are hungry to hear God's Word.

And they could not find anything that they might do, for all the people were hanging on to every word He said. (Luke 19:48)

There is an inner desire for people to hear God's Word taught, explained, and applied. People aren't turned off by the Bible; they are turned off by some who use the Bible yet whose attitudes are not right.

> And all the people would get up early in the morn-
> ing to come to Him in the temple to listen to Him.
> (Luke 21:38)

Worship is not just about us saying or singing something;
worship is, however, listening to God and listening intently for
God to speak to us, to say something to us.

Jesus included giving as an essential part of worship.

> And He sat down opposite the treasury, and began
> observing how the people were putting money into the
> treasury; and many rich people were putting in large
> sums. (Mark 12:41)

Jesus knew what everyone gave in the offering. He still does.
God does not need your money, however, you desperately need to
give it to express your faith and obedience. Jesus' looking at what
people gave in the offering was not to look at the amount but to
look at the heart. "Where your treasure is, there your heart will
be also." (Matt. 6:21)

Jesus made a promise about worship.

> "For where two or three have gathered together in
> My name, I am there in their midst." (Matt. 18:20)

The promise from Jesus is not that if two, three, or more
Christians get together that he will appear. It does mean, if
believers gather together for the express purpose and the right
motive of worshipping Jesus and allowing it to all be about him,
and allowing his agenda to be the only agenda, he has promised to
show up. It's what he wants to do. We are drawn into a spirit of
reverence, an awareness of his holiness and perfections, his
annointing for service, and his cleansing power.

What Are the Enemies of the Habit of Worship?

1.   Busyness—I'm too busy to go to church.
2.   Lack of preparedness—I'm not ready to worship.
3.   Ignorance—I'm not sure how to worship.
4.   Self-centeredness—I don't get anything out of worship.
5.   Excuses—I've got other things to do with my only day off.

FOR THE CHILDREN'S SAKE

In an article by Neil MacQueen entitled "Too Good to Be True," he offers the following: "What if I told you there was a well-researched and statistically proven program that can:

- Increase the average life expectancy of your children by 8 years.
- Significantly reduce their use and risk from Alcohol, Tobacco and Drugs.
- Dramatically reduce their risk for committing a crime.
- Improve their attitude at school and increase their school participation.
- Reduce their risk of rebelliousness.
- Reduce the likelihood that they would binge drink in college.
- Improve their odds for a 'happy' life.
- Provide them with a lifelong moral compass.
- Get them to wear their seatbelts more often.

Is there such a program? Yes, there is. And it is supported by research from Duke University, Indiana University, The University of Michigan, the Center for Disease Control, Barna Research Group, and the National Institute for Healthcare Research. What if I told you it was free, and only took about 2 hours a week. It's not a dream. The program is called 'active church participation.'"[2]

Now let's discover where we are in our generation when it comes to church attendance. Only 41 percent of Americans attend church services on a typical weekend. Each new generation becomes increasingly unchurched.[3] Parents of kids under eighteen were the most likely to say they were too busy for church.[4] "Adults who attended church regularly as a child are nearly three times as likely to be attending a church today as are their peers who avoided the church during childhood."[5] Further, Barna shows the probability of accepting Christ, segmented by age. "Children between the ages of 5 and 13 have a 32 percent probability of accepting Jesus Christ as their Savior. The probability of accepting Christ drops to 4 percent for those who are between the ages of 14 and 18. Those older than 18 have a 6 percent probability of accepting Jesus Christ as their Savior."[6] You could readily see the importance of taking a child to church. Even children from low-income neighborhoods who attend church have improved academic performances.[7]

6. Distractions—I've got too many things going on around me at the moment.
7. Bad experience—I had a bad experience in church; I was hurt, burned, offended.

Make Worship a Habit

1. Decide to be a worshipper both privately and corporately.

Nothing is more important than worshipping God daily in private worship and at least weekly in corporate worship with other believers. When worship becomes our priority, everything else lines up in the right priority.

2. Find a church that is doctrinally sound (believes, preaches, teaches the basic doctrines of faith), has life, has programs to meet the needs of your family, and is close enough for you to be involved.

Search, but don't be in slow motion about the search. It is vital to your spiritual health to find a church you can call home. This is the place of your visible commitment to Christ. To attend several churches and not be committed to one church can easily end in spiritual chaos.

3. Make a commitment that you are going to give God two hours every Sunday.

Commit at least two hours on Sunday to God. There will be exceptions, but the rule must be presence. Nothing can take the place of presence.

4. Choose to forgive if you've been hurt or burned in a past church.

Don't hold all churches hostage for one church that did you wrong. People get their feelings hurt in church, some legitimately and some not legitimately. In either case realize the church is made up of imperfect people, but the Jesus of the church is perfect. Choose to let unfaithfulness go for your own spiritual health. Not all churches are the same, so don't judge all churches by a bad experience you had in a particular church.

5. Get everything ready on Saturday night so you won't get more frustrated on Sunday morning.

This is a practical detail, but it can make all the difference on a hectic Sunday morning. Get your clothes ready on Saturday night. Form a meal game plan for Sunday. Have an agreed-upon leaving time. Protect Saturday night.

6. Pray every day for your church and church leaders.

This will make you feel close to them. It gives you a sense of connectedness to the church. Pray for the programs of the church and for your church's impact in your community.

> Worship is the highest and noblest activity of which man, by the grace of God, is capable.
> —John R. W. Stott

7. Get a good study Bible, one in which you can write notes when the message is being preached.

A good study Bible is a must. Invest some money in this. Don't be afraid to underline, circle, or highlight passages. It's OK to write in your Bible.

8. Listen to a CD of the kind of music your church offers.

Become familiar with the songs. This will help you in corporate worship on Sunday. In addition, it will create an atmosphere where you can more easily hear from God. Music is a mood setter.

9. Go to church with the idea, "This is about what I can offer to God, not about what I can get out of it."

You are there for him. You are going for God. That's why you get up when you could have slept in on Sunday morning. Keep the perspective that it's all about him. To the degree you have that attitude, you will be fulfilled in your worship experience. It's not, What did I get out of church today? but, What did I offer the Lord today in church?

10. Invite others to come to worship with you.

Many people would come to church if they were simply invited. People are interested in spiritual things. To assume otherwise is a wrong and even dangerous assumption. Anyone can invite someone to church.

THE HABIT OF
BUILDING
RELATIONSHIPS

POINT PASSAGE

*As Jesus went on from there, He saw a man called Matthew,
sitting in the tax collector's booth; and He said to him,
"Follow Me!" And he got up and followed Him. Then it happened
that as Jesus was reclining at the table in the house, behold,
many tax collectors and sinners came and were dining with
Jesus and His disciples.*
MATTHEW 9:9–10

The Jesus habit of building a relationship is taking the initiative to get to know someone—either Christian or non-Christian—beyond an acquaintance for the purpose of impact for Christ and for meeting one's personal needs for relating with others.

> More people have been brought into the church by the kindness of real Christian love than by all the theological arguments in the world.
> —**William Barclay**

Jesus Showed Us
How to Build Relationships

Jesus made a priority of building relationships with people. He knew relationship was the key to their heart. He demonstrated multiple ways to build those relationships. He taught us that the world can be changed by starting with our existing lines of relationships. Jesus built bridges to people to show them the love of

God. Jesus had close friends such as James, John, Peter, Lazarus, Mary Magdalene, and Martha. Yet to some he built a relationship for the purpose of bringing them to himself. To influence someone you must get up close.

Jesus took the initiative to build relationships.

Therefore when the Lord knew that the Pharisees had heard that Jesus was making and baptizing more disciples than John (although Jesus Himself was not baptizing, but His disciples were), He left Judea and went away again into Galilee. And He had to pass through Samaria. So He came to a city of Samaria called Sychar, near the parcel of ground that Jacob gave to his son Joseph; and Jacob's well was there. So Jesus, being wearied from His journey, was sitting thus by the well. It was about the sixth hour.

There came a woman of Samaria to draw water. Jesus said to her, "Give Me a drink." For His disciples had gone away into the city to buy food. Therefore the Samaritan woman said to Him, "How is it that You, being a Jew, ask me for a drink since I am a Samaritan woman?" (For Jews have no dealings with Samaritans.)

THE MORMONS HAVE FOUND THE SECRET

"Not everyone can teach a one-on-one Bible study. And door knocking, although it has some merit, is not the most effective way to set Bible studies or tell someone about Jesus. The Mormon church discovered this. They took a survey and discovered that the conversion rate was 0.1%. They converted only one family out of 1,000 DOORS knocked. They also discovered that the conversion rate of friendships made by people being brought into member's homes was 50%. They convert 50% of their friends. I don't agree with Mormon theology, but we can learn a lesson from them and the lesson is this: WE NEED TO MAKE FRIENDS WITH PEOPLE."[1]

Jesus answered and said to her, "If you knew the gift of God, and who it is who says to you, 'Give Me a drink,' you would have asked Him, and He would have given you living water." She said to Him, "Sir, You have nothing to draw with and the well is deep; where then do You get that living water? You are not greater than our father Jacob, are You, who gave us the well, and drank of it himself and his sons and his cattle?" Jesus answered and said to her, "Everyone who drinks of this water will thirst again; but whoever drinks of the water that I will give him shall never thirst; but the water that I will give him will become in him a well of water springing up to eternal life."

The woman said to Him, "Sir, give me this water, so I will not be thirsty nor come all the way here to draw." He said to her, "Go, call your husband and come here." The woman answered and said, "I have no husband." Jesus said to her, "You have correctly said, 'I have no husband'; for you have had five husbands, and the one whom you now have is not your husband; this you have said truly." The woman said to Him, "Sir, I perceive that You are a prophet. Our fathers worshiped in this mountain, and you people say that in Jerusalem is the place where men ought to worship." Jesus said to her, "Woman, believe Me, an hour is coming when neither in this mountain nor in Jerusalem will you worship the Father. You worship what you do not know; we worship what we know, for salvation is from the Jews. But an hour is coming, and now is, when the true worshipers will worship the Father in spirit and truth; for such people the Father seeks to be His worshipers. God is spirit, and those who worship Him must worship in spirit and truth." The woman said to Him, "I know that Messiah is coming (He who is called Christ); when that One comes, He will declare all things to us." Jesus said to her, "I who speak to you am He."

At this point His disciples came, and they were amazed that He had been speaking with a woman, yet no one said, "What do You seek?" or, "Why do You speak with her?" So the woman left her waterpot, and went into the city and said to the men, "Come, see a man who told me all the things that I have done; this is not the Christ, is it?" They went out of the city, and were coming to Him.

> You can make more friends in two months by becoming interested in other people than you can in two years by trying to get other people interested in you.
> —Dale Carnegie[2]

Meanwhile the disciples were urging Him, saying, "Rabbi, eat." But He said to them, "I have food to eat that you do not know about." So the disciples were saying to one another, "No one brought Him anything to eat, did he?" Jesus said to them, "My food is to do the will of Him who sent Me and to accomplish His work. Do you not say, 'There are yet four months, and then comes the harvest'? Behold, I say to you, lift up your eyes and look on the fields, that they are white for harvest. Already he who reaps is receiving wages and is gathering fruit for life eternal; so that he who sows and he who reaps may rejoice together. For in this case the saying is true, 'One sows and another reaps.' I sent you to reap that for which you have not labored; others have labored and you have entered into their labor."

From that city many of the Samaritans believed in Him because of the word of the woman who testified, "He told me all the things that I have done." (John 4:1–39)

Jesus approached the woman at the well. He took the initiative. He created an atmosphere of trust and love so she would drop her defenses and be open to Him. Don't wait for someone to come to you. You approach him or her. Take the first step.

Jesus didn't allow prejudice to affect his building a relationship.

As Jesus went on from there, He saw a man called Matthew, sitting in the tax collector's booth; and He said to him, "Follow Me!" And he got up and followed Him. Then it happened that as Jesus was reclining at the table in the house, behold, many tax collectors and sinners came and were dining with Jesus and His disciples. (Matt. 9:9–10)

So often what people have said about someone or a person's image prevents people from being willing to build a relationship. Jesus found out for himself. He dared to build relationships with people that the world, even the religious world, had labeled *sinners.*

Jesus demonstrated that sharing a meal is one of the best relationship builders.

He entered Jericho and was passing through. And there was a man called by the name of Zaccheus; he was a chief tax collector and he was rich. Zaccheus was trying to see who Jesus was, and was unable because of the crowd, for he was small in stature. So he ran on ahead and climbed up into a sycamore tree in order to see

---

EVERYBODY HAS SIX BASIC SPIRITUAL NEEDS

George Gallup delivered a speech at Princeton Theological Seminary in which he shared six basic spiritual needs of Americans revealed through surveys and research:

1. The need to believe that life is meaningful and has a purpose.
2. The need for a sense of community and deeper relationships.
3. The need to be appreciated and respected.
4. The need to be listened to and heard.
5. The need to feel that one is growing in faith.
6. The need for practical help in developing a mature faith.[3]

Him, for He was about to pass through that way. When Jesus came to the place, He looked up and said to him, "Zaccheus, hurry and come down, for today I must stay at your house." And he hurried and came down and received Him gladly. When they saw it, they all began to grumble, saying, "He has gone to be the guest of a man who is a sinner." Zaccheus stopped and said to the Lord, "Behold, Lord, half of my possessions I will give to the poor, and if I have defrauded anyone of anything, I will give back four times as much." And Jesus said to him, "Today salvation has come to this house, because he, too, is a son of Abraham. For the Son of Man has come to seek and to save that which was lost." (Luke 19:1–10)

Jesus went to Zaccheus's house to get to know him better. A meal provides one of the greatest settings to get to know someone. Jesus often used food as an instrument of relationship building. It sets the atmosphere for a connection with someone to take place.

Jesus didn't give up on building a relationship with someone.

But Jesus went to the Mount of Olives. Early in the morning He came again into the temple, and all the people were coming to Him; and He sat down and began to teach them. The scribes and the Pharisees brought a woman caught in adultery, and having set her in the center of the court, they said to Him, "Teacher, this woman has been caught in adultery, in the very act. Now in the Law Moses commanded us to stone such women; what then do You say?" They were saying this, testing Him, so that they might have grounds for accusing Him. But Jesus stooped down and with His finger wrote on the ground. But when they persisted in asking Him, He straightened up, and said to them, "He who is without sin among you, let him be the first to throw a stone at her." Again He stooped down and wrote on the ground. When they heard it, they began to go out one by one, beginning with the older ones, and He was left alone, and the woman, where she was, in the center of the court. Straightening up, Jesus said to her, "Woman, where are they? Did no one condemn you?" She said, "No one, Lord." And Jesus said, "I do not condemn you, either. Go. From now on sin no more." (John 8:1–11)

Jesus didn't give up on this woman caught in adultery. He looked at her as no man had ever looked at her before, with love, kindness, and truth in His eyes. Those eyes said, "I won't give up

> **Jesus had a sinner-friendly attitude.**
> **—Ron Parrish**[4]

on you, there is hope." Through relationships people can change.

Jesus confirmed that relationships are more important than structures and organizations.

A man was there who had been ill for thirty-eight years. When Jesus saw him lying there, and knew that he had already been a long time in that condition, He said to him, "Do you wish to get well?" The sick man answered Him, "Sir, I have no man to put me into the pool when the water is stirred up, but while I am coming, another steps down before me." Jesus said to him, "Get up, pick up your pallet and walk." Immediately the man became well, and picked up his pallet and began to walk. Now it was the Sabbath on that day. So the Jews were saying to the man who was cured, "It is the Sabbath, and it is not permissible for you to carry your pallet." (John 5:5–10)

With Jesus compassion came before traditions. This was just the opposite of what the religious Pharisees were demonstrating.

Jesus built a relationship in the last moments before he died.

And he was saying, "Jesus, remember me when You come in Your kingdom!" And He said to him, "Truly I say to you, today you shall be with Me in Paradise." (Luke 23:42–43)

The last thing Jesus did before He died was to build a relationship. Jesus built a relationship with one of the thieves on the cross. He changed his life. Although relationships as a rule take time to build, real relationships can be built without considerable time.

What Are the Enemies of the Habit of Relationship Building?

1. Past hurts—I have been hurt in a relationship before.
2. Pride—I'm not going to make the first move, or I don't need anyone.
3. Prejudice—I'm not going to build a relationship with that person.
4. Guilt—I have said something or done something wrong against that person.
5. Busyness—I don't have the time to build a relationship.
6. Selfishness—I will have to give up some things to build a relationship.

BLESSED ARE THE BALANCED

This is from a speech made by the CEO of Coca Cola: "Imagine life as a game in which you are juggling some five balls in the air. You name them—work, family, health, friends, and spirit—and you're keeping all of these in the air. You will soon understand that work is a rubber ball. If you drop it, it will bounce back. But the other four balls—family, health, friends, and spirit—are made of glass. If you drop any of these, they will be irrevocably scuffed, marked, nicked, damaged or even shattered. They will never be the same. You must understand that and strive for balance in your life."[5]

Make Building Relationships a Habit

1. Be yourself. Realize that some people will like you for who you are and some may not.

Don't change to attempt to get someone to like you. You are the only one like you. Yes, we can all improve what we have been given, but work on becoming the best you. God has given you a unique look and personality. Always let it be under construction as far as becoming better, but be true to you.

2. Ask every day for divine appointments in your life—people crossing your path in your daily routine.

This makes the Christian life so very exciting—anticipating what God will do in your life and the people he will bring your way during the day. You never know the divine setups God has for you. Look for them all day long.

3. Be friendly, smile, exude kindness.

Make sure your face and body language say, "I'm approachable." Often the first step in building a relationship is the way you present yourself. Be a person people like to see coming. It is not wrong to attempt to get people to like you so long as you don't compromise biblical convictions to do so.

4. Look in areas of familiarity—work, neighborhood, church, school.

Begin within your circle of influence. I am speaking of the people with whom you continually come in contact. They are there waiting for you.

5. Don't wait for someone to approach you.

Take the initiative. You might wait forever to build a relationship unless you make the first move. Take the first step. Even if you are naturally shy, take the risk. You will discover many times that the risk is worth it.

6. Focus on other people.

Listen to them. Look them in the eye. Let it all be about others. Let them know how much you are concerned about them. Make the other person feel like he or she is the most important person at that moment.

7. Be sympathetic, compassionate.

Demonstrate that you are genuinely concerned about what the other person is facing. Compassion is experiencing their pain in your heart and identifying with that pain in loving and kind ways.

8. Be there for people during times of celebration and sorrow.

Being there for people is the greatest ministry you can have to them. Nothing replaces your presence.

9. Be encouraging through words, communication, and acts of kindness.

A kind, sweet spirit can be developed by anyone. Initially, words are the greatest vehicles to express your encouragement to someone.

10. Have a good sense of humor.

Learn to laugh at yourself. Look for the light side. Be known as someone who can take a joke or enjoy one.

11. Be a giver, not a taker.

Give a Bible, a great Christian book, a CD. Realize a relationship involves giving your time and your energy. Get into the habit of giving gifts. They don't have to be expensive, just something that demonstrates that you are thinking of someone.

12. Repair broken relationships.

If you were wrong, seek to make it right. Life is too short to live in a broken relationship with someone. Do all you can to make it right, then leave it in God's hands. Be willing to do whatever is necessary to ensure that you have forgiven or sought forgiveness.

THE HABIT OF
TOUCH

POINT PASSAGE

He touched her hand, and the fever left her;
and she got up and waited on Him.

MATTHEW 8:15

The Jesus habit of touch is an appropriate physical affirmation of another person.

Your touch can bring life to someone. I'm not suggesting raising them from the dead but infusing them with life-giving encouragement. In our high-tech, take-a-number world, a touch communicates caring, concern, attention, affirmation, encouragement, and blessing.

A simple touch can disarm the defensive, defuse the negative, delight the defeated, and deliver the overwhelmed.

> Too often we underestimate the power of a touch, a smile, a kind word, a listening ear, an honest compliment, or the smallest act of caring, all of which have the potential to turn a life around.
> —Leo Buscaglia

Your touch is going to make all the difference in someone's life. It may be a pat on the back or a tap on the shoulder. It could be a high five or grabbing someone's hand to hold it or giving a handshake; perhaps it is a hug.

Jesus Showed Us How to Touch

Jesus taught us that there is power in physical touch. Throughout the Gospels we see that Jesus used human touch to make a difference in the lives of people. His touch left them encouraged, healed, changed, affirmed, and genuinely loved.

Jesus' touch healed physically.

He touched Peter's mother-in-law and made her well.

He touched her hand, and the fever left her; and she got up and waited on Him. (Matt. 8:15)

Peter had cut off the ear of a slave of the high priest. Jesus touched the ear and healed it instantly.

But Jesus answered and said, "Stop! No more of this." And He touched his ear and healed him. (Luke 22:51)

Jesus touched a leprous man, and he was immediately healed.

And He stretched out His hand and touched him, saying, "I am willing; be cleansed." And immediately the leprosy left him. (Luke 5:13)

Jesus had the healing touch. Your touch can encourage healing in people's lives.

Jesus' touch brought life.

And as Jesus returned, the people welcomed Him, for they had all been waiting for Him. And there came a man named Jairus, and he was an official of the

---

THE RESCUING HUG

The picture is called *The Rescuing Hug.* The picture warms your heart simply upon looking at it, but it inspires you beyond a warm-fuzzy when you know the story. It is the picture of premature twins with one's arm around the other. Here is the story of the first week in the life of this set of twins.

Apparently, each twin was in her respective incubator, and one was not expected to live. A hospital nurse fought against the hospital rules and placed the babies in one incubator. When they were placed together, the healthier of the two threw an arm over her sister in an endearing embrace. The smaller baby's heart rate stabilized, and her temperature rose to normal. Their Web site is http://www.daurelia.com/spirit/rescue.htm.

Hug Therapy

Touch is not only nice. It's needed. Scientific research supports the theory that stimulation by touch is absolutely necessary for our physical as well as our emotional well-being. Therapeutic touch, recognized as an essential tool for healing, is now part of nurses' training in several large medical centers. Touch is used to help relieve pain and depression and anxiety, to bolster patients' will to live, to help premature babies—who have been deprived of touch in their incubators—grow and thrive. Various experiments have shown that touch can make us feel better about ourselves and our surroundings and cause measurable physiological changes in the toucher and the touched. While there are many forms of touching, we propose that hugging is a very special one that contributes in a major way to healing and health.

Hugging
• Feels good.
• Dispels loneliness.
• Overcomes fears.
• Opens doors to feelings.
• Builds self-esteem.
• Slows down aging—huggers stay younger longer.
• Helps curb appetite—we eat less when we are nourished by hugs—and when our arms are busy wrapped around others.

Hugging also
• Eases tension.
• Fights insomnia.
• Keeps arm and shoulder muscles in condition.
• Provides stretching exercise if you are short.
• Provides stooping exercise if you are tall.
• Is democratic—anyone is eligible for a hug.

Hugging also
• Is ecologically sound—does not upset the environment.
• Is energy-efficient—saves heat; is portable.
• Requires no special equipment.
• Demands no special setting—any place from a doorstep to an executive conference room, from a church parlor to a football field, is a fine place for a hug!
• Makes happy days happier.
• Makes impossible days possible.
• Imparts feelings of belonging.
• Fills up empty places in our lives.
• Keeps on working to dispense benefits even after the hug's release.[1]

synagogue; and he fell at Jesus' feet, and began to implore Him to come to his house; for he had an only daughter, about twelve years old, and she was dying. But as He went, the crowds were pressing against Him.

And a woman who had a hemorrhage for twelve years, and could not be healed by anyone, came up behind Him and touched the fringe of His cloak, and immediately her hemorrhage stopped. And Jesus said, "Who is the one who touched Me?" And while they were all denying it, Peter said, "Master, the people are crowding and pressing in on You." But Jesus said, "Someone did touch Me, for I was aware that power had gone out of Me." When the woman saw that she had not escaped notice, she came trembling and fell down before Him, and declared in the presence of all the people the reason why she had touched Him, and how she had been immediately healed. And He said to her, "Daughter, your faith has made you well; go in peace."

> The Lockyear Principle states: "Every touch leaves an impression."

While He was still speaking, someone came from the house of the synagogue official, saying, "Your daughter has died; do not trouble the Teacher anymore." But when Jesus heard this, He answered him, "Do not be afraid any longer; only believe, and she will be made well." When He came to the house, He did not allow anyone to enter with Him, except Peter and John and James, and the girl's father and mother. Now they were all weeping and lamenting for her; but He said, "Stop weeping, for she has not died, but is asleep." And they began laughing at Him, knowing that she had died. He, however, took her by the hand and called, saying, "Child, arise!" And her spirit returned, and she got up immediately; and He gave orders for something to be given her to eat. Her parents were amazed; but He instructed them to tell no one what had happened. (Luke 8:40–56)

Jairus' daughter had died. Jesus entered the place where she was lying and took her by the hand. His touch brought life. Your touch can bring life-giving encouragement.

Jesus' touch brought hearing to the deaf.

> Jesus took him aside from the crowd, by himself,
> and put His fingers into his ears, and after spitting, He
> touched his tongue with the saliva. (Mark 7:33)

Jesus used the power of touch—putting his fingers into the ears of a deaf person—and used his own saliva and touched the man's tongue. Your touch may cause people to stop and listen—listen to you, listen to others, listen to God.

Jesus' touch brought freedom from fear.

> And Jesus came to them and touched them and said,
> "Get up, and do not be afraid." (Matt. 17:7)

On the Mount of Transfiguration, accompanied by Peter, James, and John, Jesus was transformed into a cloud of glory, and the voice of the Father frightened (terrified) the three. Jesus' touch calmed their fears. Your touch may say to someone who is afraid, "Everything is going to be OK."

Jesus' touch brought sight.

> Then He touched their eyes, saying, "It shall be done
> to you according to your faith." (Matt. 9:29)

Jesus touched the eyes of two blind men and healed them. Your touch may allow people to see things in a different light.

What Are the Enemies of the Habit of Touch?

1. Time—I just don't take the time.
2. Indifference—I just didn't think about it.
3. Upbringing—I just wasn't raised that way.
4. Fear—Someone might take it the wrong way.

Make Touch a Habit

1. Ask God every day for the opportunity to touch someone who needs it.

Be open to God guiding you to someone who needs your kind touch. He may bring unexpected people into your life or take you to unexpected places. Ask him specifically to give you divine appointments, then begin excitedly to look for them.

2. Rehearse in your mind how you can touch people.

It may be a handshake, a hug (men with men, women with women is the rule), a pat on the back, a high five, a tap on the shoulder, or grabbing a hand. Be sensitive to the situation as to what kind of touch is needed.

3. Be discerning with the opposite sex.

This is not a flirty touch. It is a quick, loving touch. One cannot be too careful when dealing with the opposite sex. It is touch in such a way that no one could ever imagine that it expresses anything other than concern.

4. Let your touch be accompanied with caring, encouraging words.

Let there be a visual/verbal connection. As you touch, let your words do the talking as to what your hands are doing.

THE HANDS OF CHRIST

During World War II, a church building in Strasbourg was destroyed. After the bombing, the members surveyed the area to see what damage was done. They were pleased that a statue of Christ with outstretched hands was still standing. It had been sculpted centuries before by a great artist. Taking a closer look, the people discovered both hands of Christ had been sheered off by a falling beam. Later, a sculptor in the town offered to replace the broken hands as a gift to the church. The church leaders met to consider the offer and decided not to accept it. They felt the statue without hands would be a great illustration that God's work is done through His people.[2]

5. Find nonphysical ways of touching, too.

You can touch people through your words, e-mails, notes, calls, or an old-fashioned handwritten letter. Sometimes it is not physically possible to touch someone. In that case, these are ways you can still accomplish touch.

6. Determine to be the hands of Christ wherever you go.

Remember the statue of the handless Christ. See yourself as an extension of Jesus Christ wherever you go. It is every Christian's responsibility.

7. Use touch to calm someone's nerves.

Touch has a calming affect on people when they are nervous. It has a way of saying, "It's going to be OK," or, "I'm here."

8. Take the power of touch to visit someone who is home-bound, in the nursing home, the hospital, retirement home, or with someone who has experienced a loss.

The great thing about touch is that it is mobile, portable. You can take it with you wherever you go. You don't have to lug around equipment, it's already there.

9. Give your wife and children a personal touch every day.

The family touch is the most important touch of all. Even if you are not from a "touchy" family, this habit can be learned. A touch with the family can break down barriers and invite them into your world.

HIGH FIVE!

It was late in the 1977 season. Dusty Baker of the Dodgers was rounding third, heading for home, having just hit his 30th home run. And the Dodgers were heading for a National League pennant. The on-deck-hitter was Glenn Burke, enjoying his second season in the big leagues. As Baker crossed the plate Burke raised his hand. Baker responded by raising his. The two hands slapped together and a bit of history was made. The first high five in baseball.[3]

10. Use the power of touch in places where people are basically seen as numbers.

Take-a-number places are everywhere. As someone has said, "We need high touch in a high-tech world." Warm up those places. Smile at people. Talk to them. Be on alert for opportunities to help them with something.

THE HABIT OF
CONFRONTATION

POINT PASSAGE

And he fell to the ground and heard a voice saying to him,
"Saul, Saul, why are you persecuting Me?" And he said,
"Who are You, Lord?" And He said, "I am Jesus whom
you are persecuting."

ACTS 9:4–5

The Jesus habit of confrontation is dealing with a person with whom there is an issue, usually negative, whether it is toward himself, others, or you, in a spirit of love and truth with the only motive being to help that person.

Jesus Showed Us How to Confront

Confrontation is often viewed as a negative word. It means to face someone about an issue, typically a sensitive issue, or some kind of problem. Now before you have visions of letting someone have it, that should be the exception, not the rule, and only after certain conditions in your own life are met. Sometimes firm action to let someone know he or she is wrong or that there is a problem is necessary. Confrontation when done in the right way—the Jesus way—becomes a platform for change.

Admittedly confrontation is difficult and uncomfortable. We

> **Truth carries with it confrontation. Truth demands confrontation: loving confrontation, but confrontation nevertheless. If our reflex action is always accommodation regardless of the centrality of the truth involved, there is something wrong.**
> **—Francis Schaeffer,**
> ***The Great Evangelical Disaster***

don't like to do it. I suppose if we did like it, we wouldn't be doing it in the right spirit. Jesus was a confronter. He dealt with problems head-on. He didn't run from uncomfortable situations. He was unwilling to allow something that was wrong to continue without saying or doing something about it. He understood that problems would not go away on their own. An intervention was necessary. Jesus' motive for confrontation was always love. Love should be the only motive for confrontation.

Jesus didn't wait to confront when the issue called for immediate attention.

> And Jesus entered the temple and drove out all those who were buying and selling in the temple, and overturned the tables of the moneychangers and the seats of those who were selling doves. (Matt. 21:12)

Jesus drove the money changers out of the temple at that moment because they were using God's house for personal gain. Jesus' confrontation always took place because it hurt God the Father or others. He didn't confront because he had been

---

A PRINCPLE FROM COACH SHULA

Don Shula, coach of the Miami Dolphins, was talking to a reporter about a player's mistake in practice. He said, "We never let an error go unchallenged. Uncorrected errors multiply."

Then the reporter said, "Isn't there benefit in overlooking one small flaw?"

Shula said, "What is a small flaw?"

I think about that all day long. What is a small flaw? I see that with my children. I've let a lot of things slide by because I was too tired. I didn't want another confrontation. But uncorrected errors do multiply. You've got to face them someday. You might as well face them on the spot. If I could do it over again with my children, I'd face the errors on the spot. It's easier on them and on you. That works in relationships with anyone. If there's something under the surface, something you sense, you might as well just bring it right out. Face it right then.[1]

offended. Sometimes confrontation must not be put off. The longer you wait, the worse it will get.

Jesus confronted Satan

Then Jesus was led up by the Spirit into the wilderness to be tempted by the devil. And after He had fasted forty days and forty nights, He then became hungry. And the tempter came and said to Him, "If You are the Son of God, command that these stones become bread." But He answered and said, "It is written, 'Man shall not live on bread alone, but on every word that proceeds out of the mouth of God.'"

Then the devil took Him into the holy city and had Him stand on the pinnacle of the temple, and said to Him, "If You are the Son of God, throw Yourself down; for it is written, 'He will command His angels concerning you'; and 'on their hands they will bear you up so that you will not strike your foot against a stone.'" Jesus said to him, "On the other hand, it is written, 'You shall not put the Lord your God to the test.'"

Again, the devil took Him to a very high mountain and showed Him all the kingdoms of the world and their glory; and he said to Him, "All these things I will give You, if You fall down and worship me." Then Jesus said to him, "Go, Satan! For it is written, 'You shall worship the Lord your God, and serve Him only.'" Then the devil left Him; and behold, angels came and began to minister to Him. (Matt. 4:1–11)

He confronted Satan in the power of the Father's strength. We have no power on our own to confront Satan, only in Jesus' name. We cannot give Satan an inch in our lives.

Jesus confronted those living in sin.

But Jesus went to the Mount of Olives. Early in the morning He came again into the temple, and all the people were coming to Him; and He sat down and began to teach them. The scribes and the Pharisees brought a woman caught in adultery, and having set her in the center of the court, they said to Him, "Teacher, this woman has been caught in adultery, in the very act. Now in the Law Moses commanded us to stone such women; what then do You say?" They were saying this, testing Him, so that they might have grounds for accusing Him. But Jesus stooped down and with His finger wrote on the ground. But when they persisted in asking Him, He straightened up, and said to them, "He who is without sin among you, let him be the first to throw a stone at her." Again He stooped down and wrote on the ground. When they heard it, they began to go out one by one, beginning with the older ones, and He was left alone, and the woman, where she was, in the center of the court. Straightening up, Jesus said to her, "Woman, where are they? Did no one condemn you?" She said, "No one, Lord." And Jesus said, "I do not condemn you, either. Go. From now on sin no more." (John 8:1–11)

Jesus confronted this woman living in sin, but he also confronted the self-righteous Pharisees for their sinful attitude. There are times when we must confront people about their living in sin.

Jesus confronted his family.

When the wine ran out, the mother of Jesus said to Him, "They have no wine." And Jesus said to her, "Woman, what does that have to do with us? My hour has not yet come." His mother said to the servants, "Whatever He says to you, do it." (John 2:3–5)

Then, after three days they found Him in the temple, sitting in the midst of the teachers, both listening to them and asking them questions. And all who heard Him were amazed at His understanding and His answers. When they saw Him, they were astonished; and His mother said to Him, "Son, why have You treated us this way? Behold, Your father and I have been anxiously looking for You."

And He said to them, "Why is it that you were looking for
Me? Did you not know that I had to be in My Father's
house?" (Luke 2:46–49)

When Jesus' earthly family got in
the way of his putting his heavenly Father
first, he confronted them. There are
times you may need to confront your
family when your family attempts to get
you to put anything else ahead of God.

> You must live with
> people to know their
> problems, and live
> with God in order to
> solve them.
> —Peter T. Forsyth

Jesus confronted Martha, who was putting things ahead of him.

Now as they were traveling along, He entered a village; and a woman named Martha welcomed Him into
her home. She had a sister called Mary, who was seated
at the Lord's feet, listening to His word. But Martha was
distracted with all her preparations; and she came up to
Him and said, "Lord, do You not care that my sister has
left me to do all the serving alone? Then tell her to help
me." But the Lord answered and said to her, "Martha,
Martha, you are worried and bothered about so many
things; but only one thing is necessary, for Mary has
chosen the good part, which shall not be taken away
from her." (Luke 10:38–42)

Jesus let Martha know that her busyness and activity—as
commendable as that might have been—must never be put in
front of worshipping him.

Jesus confronted Saul on the road to Damascus.

And he fell to the ground and heard a voice saying to
him, "Saul, Saul, why are you persecuting Me?" And he
said, "Who are You, Lord?" And He said, "I am Jesus
whom you are persecuting." (Acts 9:4–5)

Jesus confronted Saul who had persecuted his own. His confrontation of "Saul you are wrong" gave him an opportunity to
come to faith in him.

Jesus confronted the self-righteous Pharisees, who used religion and God for their own purposes.

"Woe to you, scribes and Pharisees, hypocrites! For you clean the outside of the cup and of the dish, but inside they are full of robbery and self-indulgence. You blind Pharisee, first clean the inside of the cup and of the dish, so that the outside of it may become clean also. Woe to you, scribes and Pharisees, hypocrites! For you are like whitewashed tombs which on the outside appear beautiful, but inside they are full of dead men's bones and all uncleanness." (Matt. 23:25–27)

He minced no words, especially to those who used God for personal gain and for controlling others. When religious activity is placed above a relationship with Christ, confrontation is necessary.

Jesus confronted Peter for allowing Satan to suggest through him that he should bypass the cross.

From that time Jesus began to show His disciples that He must go to Jerusalem, and suffer many things from the elders and chief priests and scribes, and be killed, and be raised up on the third day. Peter took Him aside and began to rebuke Him, saying, "God forbid it, Lord! This shall never happen to You." But He turned and said to Peter, "Get behind Me, Satan! You are a stumbling block to Me; for you are not setting your mind on God's interests, but man's." (Matt. 16:21–23)

Jesus saw past the surface and got at the heart of the suggestion. He knew it was from Satan. There are times when we must look beyond what someone says and understand it may be coming from the enemy.

Jesus confronted God, the Father, when he was on the cross.

About the ninth hour Jesus cried out with a loud voice, saying, "Eli, Eli, lama sabachthani?" that is, "My

God, My God, why have you forsaken me?" (Matt. 27:46)

Jesus was honest enough with God the Father to ask him "why?" There are times in our humanity that we may feel disappointed with God. Expressing that to God is not wrong.

What Are the Enemies of the Habit of Confrontation?

1. Fear—I'm afraid of how the other person will respond.
2. Procrastination—Not now, I'll wait and see.
3. Assumption—Maybe it will get better.
4. Abdication—Let someone else do it.

Make Confrontation a Habit

This is not to suggest that you become a spiritual policeman, looking for opportunities to let someone have it but being willing to confront issues when necessary.

1. Make sure your own heart is right with God before you confront someone.

This is Jesus' get-the-log-out-of-your-own-eye teaching. Deal with your log first. Jesus isn't suggesting that you never confront anyone, quite the contrary. He tells us first to get our lives right so we can see to help others more clearly with the right motive.

2. Pray for the person that needs to be confronted.

Make that person a target of your praying. Intercede for that person prior to confronting him. Prayer creates the atmosphere where real change can take place.

3. Set up a time with the person to talk, in private without interruption, but don't put it off.

Do it as soon as possible. Never confront in front of others or in any kind of public place. Your intention is to help, not to embarrass in any way. The right timing is imperative.

4. When the occasion calls for it, confront immediately.

Stand up and speak up for what is right and stand up and speak up against wrong. Immediate confrontation is sometimes necessary. The moment demands it in order to set things right in the minds of other people as well.

5. Don't take out your own anger on someone.

This is not an occasion for you to vent your own anger or frustration at the other person. Make sure your confrontation is not about telling someone off.

6. Begin with a word of encouragement.

Always start on a positive note. Encourage the person. You don't want to put the person immediately on the defensive.

7. Ask the person, "If I could share something with you that would help you, would you want me to?"

This gives you permission to share. If the person says yes, then share the problem. If the person says no, trust God that the person will change his attitude. This question can really turn things around.

8. State the issue as you see it.

Give your perspective of the issue. Say, "This is the way I see it, please help me to understand." Admit that maybe you misunderstood or got the wrong perspective.

9. Ask how you can help the person.

Genuinely let the person know that you are only there to help him. Make sure the person understands your motive is out of love for him, not to hurt him.

10. Be confidential.

Never betray a confidence. You will blow it every time and do much more damage if you share a confidence.

11. Pray for the person.

Pray for the person right there. Let your prayer reflect your genuine desire for the Lord to use this time and for Satan not to take advantage.

THE HABIT OF
CHALLENGING
THE STATUS QUO

POINT PASSAGE

"Neglecting the commandment of God,
you hold to the tradition of men."
MARK 7:8

The Jesus habit of challenging the status quo is choosing to challenge, in a spirit of love, that which continues on, usually based on tradition, with no purpose.

> If your horse is dead, for goodness sakes—dismount.
> —Eddy Ketchursid

Jesus Showed Us How to Challenge the Status Quo

The status quo is simply the way things are. *"Que sera sera, whatever will be, will be."*[1] Jesus showed the world they didn't have to live a just-barely-getting-by kind of life. He showed the abundant, utmost, kind of life that anyone could live. Jesus challenged tradition that had no meaning or benefit (Matt. 15:1–3; Mark 7:8). Jesus was zealously committed to upholding God's commands and laws, yet he challenged man-made rules that were controlling people's lives.

Jesus talked to a woman, a Samaritan, which was against tradition.

Therefore the Samaritan woman said to Him, "How is it thatYou, being a Jew, ask me for a drink since I am

a Samaritan woman?" (For Jews have no dealings with
Samaritans.) (John 4:9)

Jesus confronted wrongful prejudice. The woman and her
needs were more important to Jesus than recognizing man-made
limitations.

Jesus healed on the sabbath, which was against tradition.

> They were watching Him to see if He would heal
> him on the Sabbath, so that they might accuse Him. The
> Pharisees went out and immediately began conspiring
> with the Herodians against Him, as to how they might
> destroy Him. (Mark 3:2, 6)

Again, the needs of the person became more important to
Jesus than keeping the letter of the law.

Jesus befriended sinners.

> "The Son of Man came eating and drinking, and they
> say, 'Behold a gluttonous man and a drunkard, a friend
> of tax-gatherers and sinners!' Yet wisdom is vindicated
> by her deeds." (Matt. 11:19)

Jesus loved sinners and reached out to them instead of con-
demning them as hopeless. This made the Pharisees angry.

THE COTTON IN THE BOTTLE OF ASPIRIN

Bayer Corporation has stopped putting the cotton wads in their Genuine Bayer bottles. The company realized the aspirin would hold up fine without the maddening white clumps, which it had included since about 1914. "We concluded there really wasn't any reason to keep the cotton except tradition," said Chris Allen, Bayer's vice president of technical operations. "Besides, it's hard to get out."[2]

THE COSTLY REFUSAL
TO CHANGE

"Of the twenty largest companies in the U.S. forty years ago, only two are still among the first twenty in size. Of the one hundred largest companies twenty-five years ago, almost half have disappeared or have declined substantially from their peak." Refusal to change spells decline.[3]

What Are the Enemies of the Habit of Challenging the Status Quo?

1.   Comfort—I'm used to it.
2.   Resistance—I don't want to change.
3.   Laziness—It takes too much effort to change.
4.   Mind-set—Nothing's going to change.

Make Challenging the Status Quo a Habit

1. Begin with the belief that things can change.

> In matters of style, swim with the current. In matters of principle, stand like a rock.
> **—Unknown**

Jesus came out of the grave so things wouldn't have to remain the same. There is power to change. Only those who choose not to change, don't change. There is no problem that cannot be transformed by a resurrected Jesus Christ.

2. Don't accept what others have said about something being too difficult or impossible.

There are always people to tell you why things won't work. You will encounter negative people everywhere you go. Many times, because they are not willing to pay the price for change, they will attempt to infuse a situation with enough of the negative that it throws cold water on your enthusiasm. You simply cannot listen to those people.

3. Set goals as to the way you want things to be.

Goal setting is powerful. Writing it down becomes the first point in changing things. It is a fact that we tend to do those things we write down more than if we had not written them down.

4. Have the "and then some" philosophy of life.

Don't settle for average. Go the extra mile. Do more than is necessary. Never get to the point where you are just simply getting by in life. Don't always be looking for the shortcuts and loopholes. Give everything your enthusiastic best.

5. Challenge the way things are if they are not the way they should be.

Dare to be a change agent. Let God use you to make a difference. You can do it in love and with tactfulness. God may want to use you as the one who would make a difference. Make sure that what you desire to change is worth the effort it will take to change it.

THINKING OUTSIDE THE BOX

In Mark Eppler's book, *The Wright Way*, he shows how Orville and Wilbur Wright bucked the status-quo mind-set of their day by attempting to build a heavier-than-air flying machine. One step of their problem-solving technique is called "mind warping." Mind warping is "the ability to think outside the box, without abandoning the box." Participants often describe the box as:

- The status quo—the pressure on all sides to keep things the way they are.
- Root bound—having no room to grow and no chance of being transplanted.
- Tradition—long ago someone decided . . .
- Groupthink—if you need an idea, we'll tell you what it is.
- Rigid thinking—an unbending attitude.
- A pen—an enclosure.
- A pine box—where creativity goes to die.[4]

Christians are people God has called to think outside the box, without abandoning our core beliefs.

6. Discover what obstacles you would face if you challenged the way things are.

Ask yourself, "If I attempt this change, what specifically am I going to have to overcome?" Anticipate the negative. Accept that changing the status quo will not be easy.

7. List the areas of your life that have grown stagnant.

We all have a tendency to grow stagnant, to follow the path of least resistance. Specifically target those areas where you no longer feel you are growing.

8. Don't change just for the sake of change.

Have a real purpose in attempting to change things. Change sometimes is not the best. To change without a purpose is to invite confusion. Some things are best left unchanged. Ask yourself, "Why do I feel this needs to change?"

> Lord, give me the grace to recognize the things which cannot be changed, courage to change those which can, and wisdom to know the difference.
> —Unknown

9. Be kind in challenging the status quo.

Don't go in with a prideful attitude that turns people off. You can easily offend people. Change comes so much easier when presented in an atmosphere of kindness. Sometimes it's not the idea of change that bothers people but the way in which that change is presented.

10. Give it time!

Change takes time. Be patient. Hang in there. Some days you make great strides, but other days seem slow. Don't give up. Remember, the process of challenging the status quo can bring your greatest sense of fulfillment.

THE HABIT OF
LISTENING

POINT PASSAGE

There came a woman of Samaria to draw water.
Jesus said to her, "Give Me a drink." For His disciples had
gone away into the city to buy food. Therefore the Samaritan
woman said to Him, "How is it that You, being a Jew, ask me
for a drink since I am a Samaritan woman?" (For Jews have
no dealings with Samaritans.)

JOHN 4:7–9

The Jesus habit of listening is focusing on what another person is saying with your ears, mind, eyes, and body, making that person feel valued by you.

> *People will rarely remember your advice, but they will remember that you listened.*
> **—Cara Lawrence**

Jesus Showed Us How to Listen

Jesus was the consummate listener. He still is. Imagine all those prayers he continues to listen to—from people all around the world, 24–7. Jesus listened not only with his ears but also with his eyes, his mind, and his body. People that were speaking to him had his full attention at that moment. He zoned in on that person. By listening he made people feel they had value.

Jesus listened to the rich young ruler.

Looking at him, Jesus felt a love for him and said to him, "One thing you lack: go and sell all you possess and give to the poor, and you will have treasure in heaven; and come, follow Me." (Mark 10:21)

Jesus looked intently into the eyes of this man who was trying to find a shortcut to eternal life. He didn't simply put him off; he listened. That man left unsaved, but he left knowing he had been heard. People need to leave us feeling they have been heard. We may not agree with them or acquiesce to their way of thinking, but we have listened.

Jesus listened to an intellectual.

Now there was a man of the Pharisees, named Nicodemus, a ruler of the Jews; this man came to Jesus by night and said to Him, "Rabbi, we know that You have come from God as a teacher; for no one can do these signs that You do unless God is with him." Jesus answered and said to him, "Truly, truly, I say to you, unless one is born again he cannot see the kingdom of God."

Nicodemus said to Him, "How can a man be born when he is old? He cannot enter a second time into his mother's womb and be born, can he?" Jesus answered, "Truly, truly, I say to you, unless one is born of water and the Spirit he cannot enter into the kingdom of God. That which is born of the flesh is flesh, and that which is born

BLIND MAN CLIMBS MT. EVEREST

Erik Weihenmayer is blind, yet on May 25, 2001 (Nepal time), he reached the peak of Mt. Everest. Suffering from a degenerative eye disease, he lost his sight when he was thirteen, but that didn't stop him. On a mountain where 90 percent of the climbers never make it to the top—165 have died trying since 1953—Erik succeeded, in large measure because he listened well. He listened to the little bell tied to the back of the climber in front of him so he would know what direction to go. He listened to the voice of teammates who would shout back to him, "Death fall two feet to your right!" He listened to the sound of his pick jabbing the ice so he would know whether the ice was safe to cross.[1]

of the Spirit is spirit. Do not be amazed that I said to you, 'You must be born again.' The wind blows where it wishes and you hear the sound of it, but do not know where it comes from and where it is going; so is everyone who is born of the Spirit."

> *What people really need is a good listening to.*
> —**Mary Lour Casey**

Nicodemus said to Him, "How can these things be?" Jesus answered and said to him, "Are you the teacher of Israel and do not understand these things? Truly, truly, I say to you, we speak of what we know and testify of what we have seen, and you do not accept our testimony. If I told you earthly things and you do not believe, how will you believe if I tell you heavenly things? No one has ascended into heaven, but He who descended from heaven: the Son of Man. As Moses lifted up the serpent in the wilderness, even so must the Son of Man be lifted up; so that whoever believes will in Him have eternal life.

"For God so loved the world, that He gave His only begotten Son, that whoever believes in Him shall not perish, but have eternal life." (John 3:1–16)

Nicodemus came at night to talk with Jesus. He was an intellectual. Jesus didn't argue with him; he did listen to him, heard him out, and then shared the truth with him. Our listening earns us the right to share with a person.

Jesus listened to the woman at the well.

There came a woman of Samaria to draw water. Jesus said to her, "Give Me a drink." For His disciples had gone away into the city to buy food. Therefore the Samaritan woman said to Him, "How is it that You, being a Jew, ask me for a drink since I am a Samaritan woman?" (For Jews have no dealings with Samaritans.) (John 4:7–9)

Jesus listened with love and care to this woman who had been used and abused by men. His listening brought her to the point of

receiving him personally. The world will be more open to our message of the gospel if we will first listen with love to their hurts.

Jesus listened to the man at the pool of Bethesda.

> After these things there was a feast of the Jews, and
> Jesus went up to Jerusalem.
>
> Now there is in Jerusalem by the sheep gate a pool,
> which is called in Hebrew Bethesda, having five porti-
> coes. In these lay a multitude of those who were sick,
> blind, lame, and withered, waiting for the moving of the
> waters; for an angel of the Lord went down at certain
> seasons into the pool and stirred up the water; whoever
> then first, after the stirring up of the water, stepped in
> was made well from whatever disease with which he
> was afflicted. A man was there who had been ill for
> thirty-eight years. When Jesus saw him lying there, and
> knew that he had already been a long time in that con-
> dition, He said to him, "Do you wish to get well?" The
> sick man answered Him, "Sir, I have no man to put me
> into the pool when the water is stirred up, but while
> I am coming, another steps down before me." Jesus said
> to him, "Get up, pick up your pallet and walk."
> Immediately the man became well, and picked up his
> pallet and began to walk. Now it was the Sabbath on
> that day. (John 5:1–9)

The man had been lame for thirty-eight years. Jesus stopped
and listened to this man and healed him. Our listening can bring
healing to people's hurts.

Jesus listened to the Syrophoenician woman.

> Jesus got up and went away from there to the region
> of Tyre. And when He had entered a house, He wanted
> no one to know of it; yet He could not escape notice.
> But after hearing of Him, a woman whose little daugh-
> ter had an unclean spirit immediately came and fell at
> His feet. Now the woman was a Gentile, of the

Syrophoenician race. And she kept asking Him to cast the demon out of her daughter. And He was saying to her, "Let the children be satisfied first, for it is not good to take the children's bread and throw it to the dogs." But she answered and said to Him, "Yes, Lord, but even the dogs under the table feed on the children's crumbs." And He said to her, "Because of this answer go; the demon has gone out of your daughter." And going back to her home, she found the child lying on the bed, the demon having left. (Mark 7:24–30)

This woman's daughter possessed a demon. Jesus took the time to listen to her and cast the demon out of her little girl. People all around us are hurting. A listening ear can make all the difference. It may be that God places you at the right place, at the right time, to do something about it.

Jesus listened to children.

And they were bringing children to Him so that He might touch them; but the disciples rebuked them. But when Jesus saw this, He was indignant and said to them, "Permit the children to come to Me; do not hinder them; for the kingdom of God belongs to such as these. Truly I say to you, whoever does not receive the kingdom of God like a child will not enter it at all." And He took them in His arms and began blessing them, laying His hands on them. (Mark 10:13–16)

I JUST NEED FOR YOU TO LISTEN

Teenage prostitutes, during interviews in a San Francisco study, were asked: "Is there anything you needed most and couldn't get?" Their response, invariably preceded by sadness and tears was unanimous: "What I needed most was someone to listen to me. Someone who cared enough to listen to me."[2]

Jesus didn't dismiss children, quite the opposite. He listened to them. He took time to hear what they were saying. Children are precious to Jesus. We must take the time to listen to what their little hearts are trying to express. It makes them feel valued, and we just might learn something ourselves.

What Are the Enemies of the Habit of Listening?

1. Busyness—I just don't have time to listen.
2. Distractions—Is that my cell phone? I wonder what's being said over there?

> *The first duty of love is to listen.* —**Paul Tillich**

3. Lack of interest—I just don't care what this person is saying.
4. Selfishness—I want to talk about me!

Make Listening a Habit

1. When you are with someone, make that person your focus.

Let the person feel that he or she is the most important thing to you. It is the "you matter" factor.

2. Neglect everything else and everyone else around you for that moment.

This is planned neglect. You plan to neglect everything else around you so that you can give your full attention to that person. People need to be taught to respect your focus.

3. Look directly at the person in the eyes.

You will be amazed at the power of simply focusing on a person's eyes when it comes to listening. The eyes are the windows to the soul.

4. Don't be looking around at other people.

Make eye contact. At that moment nobody else matters except the person who is talking.

5. Watch facial expressions, body language, and tone.

You can learn much from a person's nonverbal cues. In fact you may even learn more. Pay close attention.

6. Forget your cell phone for the moment.

Put away anything that could hinder you from listening to that person. Today cell phones seem to be the greatest culprit of good listening. We got by when we didn't have cell phones, and for that moment when someone is talking to us, we can get by without them again.

7. Position your body in a way that says, "I am focusing on you at this moment."

Your body language indicates the degree to which you are listening. The other person will notice.

8. Don't be thinking about what you are going to say in response to what the person is saying.

You will miss hearing key thoughts and words if you do. We must put that person's need for a listening ear ahead of our desire to talk.

9. Ask questions for clarification and to keep conversation on track.

Don't let the conversation wander all over creation. Use a question or make a response to keep or get things back on track.

10. Don't prejudge, making up your mind about what the person is going to say before he or she says it.

Give the person the freedom to tell you what they he wants to say. Don't listen with the attitude of, "I already know what you will say, so I'm going to respond accordingly." That is a form of prejudice—prejudging what you think the person will say. Not only will you run the risk of missing the person's point, but you can end up embarrassing yourself.

11. Listen for what is not said.

Peter Drucker said, "The most important thing in communication is to hear what isn't being said."[3]

What is not said can speak volumes about the needs and attitudes of that person. That is third-ear listening.

THE HABIT OF
LOVE

*"Just as the Father has loved Me,
I have also loved you; abide in My love."*
JOHN 15:9

The Jesus habit of love is choosing consistently to do something that is beneficial, kind, and encouraging for someone before considering your own needs and being willing to be inconvenienced and to sacrifice for the sake of others.

> Human love says,
> "I will love you if . . ."
> God says, "I will love
> you even . . ."
> —**Stuart Briscoe**

Jesus Showed Us How to Love

Love is one of those words that has been used so much, and so often abused, that its meaning is easily lost. No other word has been so written about, talked about, reported on, or sung about. Our society has a tendency, however, to group *love* with sex, food, clothes, people, or some emotional, warm fuzzy feeling. This confusion about love often shows up in marriage.

Jesus loved people. One has to look no further than the cross to see that love displayed. He loved people all of the time. His love was unconditional—a no-matter-what-you-have-done, no-matter-where-you-have-been, no-matter-who-you-are, self-giving, self-sacrificing kind of love. He told us that it would become the distinguishing mark of those who know Him.

"By this all men will know that you are My disciples,
if you have love for one another." (John 13:35)

Jesus loved the lovable.

Now Jesus loved Martha and her sister and Lazarus. (John 11:5)

When Jesus then saw His mother, and the disciple whom He loved standing nearby, He said to His mother, "Woman, behold, your son!" (John 19:26)

He loved people who loved him and never took them for granted. Sometimes we take for granted those who love us most.

UNEXPECTED LOVE

Former televangelist Jim Bakker speaks of events that occurred immediately after his release from prison: When I was transferred to my last prison, Franklin Graham said he wanted to help me when I got out—with a job, a house to live in, and a car. It was my fifth Christmas in prison. I thought it over and said, "Franklin, you can't do this. It will hurt you. The Grahams don't need my baggage." He looked at me and said, "Jim, you were my friend in the past, and you are my friend now. If anyone doesn't like it, I'm looking for a fight."

So when I got out of prison, the Grahams sponsored me and paid for a house for me to live in and gave me a car to drive. The first Sunday out, Ruth Graham called the halfway house I was living in at the Salvation Army and asked permission for me to go to the Montreat Presbyterian Church with her that Sunday morning. When I got there, the pastor welcomed me and sat me with the Graham family. There were like two whole rows of them—I think every Graham aunt and uncle and cousin was there. The organ began playing, and the place was full except for a seat next to me. Then the doors opened and in walked Ruth Graham. She walked down that aisle and sat next to inmate 07407-058. I had only been out of prison for forty-eight hours, but she told the world that morning that Jim Bakker was her friend.

Afterward, she had me up to their cabin for dinner. When she asked me for some addresses, I pulled this envelope out of my pocket to look for them—in prison you're not allowed to have a wallet, so you just carry an envelope. She asked, "Don't you have a wallet?" And I said, "Well, yeah, this is my wallet." After five years of brainwashing in prison, you think an envelope is a wallet. She walked into the other room and came back and said, "Here's one of Billy's wallets. He doesn't need it. You can have it."[1]

Jesus wasn't afraid to express his love to people.

> "A new commandment I give to you, that you love one another, even as I have loved you, that you also love one another." (John 13:34)

Jesus told people, "I love you." We must learn to express to people that we love them. Telling them is of utmost importance.

Jesus loved the unlovable.

> One of the criminals who were hanged there was hurling abuse at Him, saying, "Are You not the Christ? Save Yourself and us!" But the other answered, and rebuking him said, "Do you not even fear God, since you are under the same sentence of condemnation? And we indeed are suffering justly, for we are receiving what we deserve for our deeds; but this man has done nothing wrong." And he was saying, "Jesus, remember me when You come in Your kingdom!" And He said to him, "Truly I say to you, today you shall be with Me in Paradise." (Luke 23:39–43)

Jesus loved the thief on the cross. He loved people who were difficult to love. It is a testimony to our relationship with Jesus when we love those that are not lovable.

Jesus loved his enemies.

> And said, "What are you willing to give me to betray Him to you?" And they weighed out thirty pieces of silver to him. (Matt. 26:15)

> While He was still speaking, behold, Judas, one of the twelve, came up accompanied by a large crowd with

---

LOVE ON AMAZON.COM

Love is a popular word in our society. Amazon.com lists:

- 2,652 book titles about heaven
- 10,304 about money
- 16,765 about sex
- 18,818 about God
- 30,066 about love[2]

swords and clubs, who came from the chief priests and elders of the people. Now he who was betraying Him gave them a sign, saying, "Whomever I kiss, He is the one; seize Him." Immediately Judas went to Jesus and said, "Hail, Rabbi!" and kissed Him. And Jesus said to him, "Friend, do what you have come for." Then they came and laid hands on Jesus and seized Him. (Matt. 26:47–50)

> To love someone means to see him as God intended him.
> —Fyodor Dostoyevsky

Jesus loved Judas even after he had sold him for thirty pieces of silver, roughly $5,000. Love is the only power we can have over our enemies.

Jesus showed us that love is a choice.

"Or do you think that I cannot appeal to My Father, and He will at once put at My disposal more than twelve legions of angels?" (Matt. 26:53)

Jesus chose to stay on the cross. It was the choice of love. He could have called down as many as seventy-two thousand angels and obliterated his enemies and come down off the cross. He demonstrated that love is not a feeling.

What Are the Enemies of the Habit of Love?

1. Ignorance—Love is a feeling. Love means never having to say you're sorry. Love is sex.
2. Selfishness—I want my needs met. Me first.
3. Indifference—It doesn't matter to me.

Make Love a Habit

1. Realize that love is not a feeling, so you don't have to possess a certain feeling.

To equate love with a feeling is to invite discouragement. If love was based on a feeling, love would be inconsistent. Love seen only as feeling is limited and is not love at all.

2. Love is a choice you make.

Love is an act of your will. It is something you decide to do. "I choose to love you." You could choose not to as well, but be sure, it is a choice.

3. Love is something you do.

Love expresses itself in action. Real love is demonstrated consistently in practical ways. You can always spot real love because it doesn't just sit there.

> People don't go where the action is, they go where love is.
> —Jess Moody

4. Choosing to do the right thing toward someone, as a habit, will bring the right feelings.

This will work. If you wait until you feel like it before you do the right thing, you will probably never do the right thing. However, if you choose to do what is right toward someone, emotions will follow.

5. Determine to show people love no matter what they do to you or say to you.

Let love be your response. This kind of love will more than likely, over time, win people over. There is nothing that shows real Christianity like love. It is amazing how disarming it is to respond to those who are not acting in love, when you demonstrate the love of God. It lets them know that you are different when they don't get a typical, hateful response.

LOVE: IS IT FOR THE BIRDS?

"Love can be wonderful, but it also can be destructive. It can cause people to lie, to cheat, to commit murder, and—worst of all—to write lyrics like these: 'Why do birds suddenly appear, Every time you are near?' These lyrics are, of course, from the Carpenters' huge hit, 'Close to You.' You frankly have to ask yourself: 'Do I really want to be near somebody who causes birds to appear suddenly? Didn't Alfred Hitchcock do a horror movie about this?'"[3]

6. Learn to express your love to people.

Work on ways to let people know you love them. Tell people, "I love you." That may be uncomfortable at first, but it will get easier. In fact, it is contagious.

7. Understand that there is no way to experience agape (unconditional) love outside of a relationship with Jesus Christ.

When you become a Christian, it opens up a whole new God-dimension of love. One's capacity to love this way is limited to real Christianity.

> Love so amazing, so divine, demands my soul my life, my all.
> —Isaac Watts

8. Realize the world's definition of love and God's definition are different.

The world has attached every kind of definition to the word *love*. Often it is used in purely sensual terms. Yet only God's definition of *love* satisfies the inner vacuum of the human soul. His kind of love alone brings life.

9. Do a loving action toward someone who has hurt or offended you.

This will help free you from the bondage of bitterness. This is the Jesus factor, choosing to bless instead of blister someone who has wounded you.

10. Recognize that love is the element that creates an atmosphere where change can take place.

If you want people to change, love them. Love creates an environment, the kind that allows people the freedom to become more like Jesus Christ. Where there is love, miracles can take place and transformations can occur.

THE HABIT OF
THANKFULNESS

POINT PASSAGE

And when He had taken a cup and given thanks,
He gave it to them, saying, "Drink from it, all of you."
MATTHEW 26:27

The Jesus habit of thankfulness is the continual choice you make to be grateful to God in any situation with the belief that God is greater than that situation.

> **The hardest arithmetic to master is that which enables us to count our blessings.**
> **—Eric Hoffer**

Jesus Showed Us How to Be Thankful

Jesus lived in a spirit of thankfulness to the Father. He never took the blessings of God for granted. He continually took the time to stop and thank his Father. Jesus was not a complainer.

Jesus blessed the food before the miracles of the feeding of the five thousand.

Ordering the people to sit down on the grass, He took the five loaves and the two fish, and looking up toward heaven, He blessed the food, and breaking the loaves He gave them to the disciples, and the disciples gave them to the crowds. (Matt. 14:19)

Jesus thanked God in advance for the miracle. Being thankful can bring miracles in your life. Thankfulness to God releases the power of faith, which releases the power of God into a circumstance or need.

Jesus blessed the food before the feeding of the four thousand.

> And He took the seven loaves and the fish; and giv-
> ing thanks, He broke them and started giving them to
> the disciples, and the disciples gave them to the people.
> (Matt. 15:36)

Jesus, through his thankfulness, announced that God the Father would provide. Thankfulness puts it in God's hands, turning it over to a turn-it-around God.

Jesus blessed the food before the last supper.

> While they were eating, Jesus took some bread, and
> after a blessing, He broke it and gave it to the disciples,
> and said, "Take, eat; this is My body." And when He had
> taken a cup and given thanks, He gave it to them, say-
> ing, "Drink from it, all of you." (Matt. 26:26–27)

Jesus was thankful even though he was about to face the greatest crisis of his life, in fact, the greatest crisis in history. A spirit of thankfulness prepares us to face life's darkest hours. It puts God in control, instead of us.

SO YOU THINK A GALLON OF GASOLINE IS EXPENSIVE?

- Diet Snapple 16 oz for $1.29=$10.32 per gallon.
- Lipton Iced Tea 16 oz for $1.19=$9.52 per gallon.
- Gatorade 10 oz for $1.59=$10.17 per gallon.
- Ocean Spray 16 oz for $1.25=$10.00 per gallon.
- STP Brake Fluid 12 oz for $3.15= $33.60 per gallon.
- Vick's Nyquil 6 oz for $8.35=$178.13 per gallon.

- Pepto-Bismol 4 oz for $3.85=$123.20 per gallon.
- White-Out 7 oz for $1.39=$25.42 per gallon.
- Scope 1.5 oz for $0.99=$84.48 per gallon.
  And this is the final kicker . . .
- Evian water 9 oz for $1.49=$21.19 per gallon.
  So the next time you're at the pump, be glad your car doesn't run on Nyquil, Scope, or Whiteout![1]

Jesus blessed the food in the home of the two disciples on the road to Emmaus.

> When He had reclined at the table with them, He took the bread and blessed it, and breaking it, He began giving it to them. (Luke 24:30)

As Jesus broke the bread and gave thanks to the Father, something caused them to know who he was. His thankfulness revealed who he was. Perhaps as he was thanking God and breaking the bread, they saw the nail prints still in his hands. When you are thankful, you reveal *whose* you are. It lets the world see a glimpse of Christ.

Jesus thanked the Father before raising Lazarus from the dead

> So they removed the stone. Then Jesus raised His eyes, and said, "Father, I thank You that You have heard Me." (John 11:41)

His thankfulness was an act of faith that demonstrated God's intervention. Thankfulness is an expression to God that says, "I believe you will come through."

What Are the Enemies of the Habit of Thankfulness?

1. Complaining—Why can't something good happen to me?

THIS TOO SHALL PASS

Scottish minister Alexander Whyte was known for his uplifting prayers in the pulpit. He always found something for which to be grateful. One Sunday morning the weather was so gloomy that one church member thought to himself, "Certainly the preacher won't think of anything for which to thank God on a wretched day like this." Much to his surprise, however, Whyte began by praying. "We thank Thee, O God, that it is not always like this."[2]

2. Taking God's blessing for granted—What have you done for me lately?
3. Lack of faith—What if God doesn't come through?
4. Pessimism—It's not all good.
5. Selfishness—Why does that person have more than I have?

Make Thankfulness a Habit

1. Thankfulness is a choice, not a feeling—choose it!

You can choose to have an attitude of gratitude. Start thanking God for your blessings rather than complaining about what you don't have. Focus on the goodness of God in your life.

2. Look past the circumstances and look to the one who has the power to change everything.

Gazing at your circumstances will lead you to despair. Not only look past your circumstances, but look

Certainly a marked feature of Christ's character was his perennial gratefulness of spirit. Run through His prayers and you will be surprised how large a place thanksgiving holds in them, how often He gave eager praise for what would have soured you and me. And made us feel quite certain that God had forgotten to be gracious. Did He not take the cup, that awful symbol of things so near and so fearsome, and even then give thanks?
—A. J. Gossip, from
The Edge of the Crowd

above them. Someone commented that he was under his circumstances. The other person said, "What in the world are you doing under there?" Thankfulness moves you out from under your circumstances.

3. See every problem as an opportunity for God to be God.

Every obstacle you face is an invitation for God to get involved. Thank him that he is bigger that the circumstance you are facing. You are not feeling grateful for everything that happens; you are simply choosing to believe God is greater.

4. Replace complaining with thankfulness.

Every time you have a tendency to start complaining, immediately exchange it with thanksgiving to God. This is "complaint replacement therapy."

5. Begin the day with thanking God that you are given another day to live.

Get up thanking God that you have been given another day to live, another day to make a difference. This is the greatest way to begin your day. Start the day off right.

6. Look around and realize that there is always someone who has it more difficult than you.

You don't have to look long to discover just how blessed you are. Every day you see people who have more trouble, more struggles, and tougher situations than you.

7. Spend time with thankful, positive people.

Surround yourself with grateful people. Their thankfulness will be contagious. Stay away, as much as possible, from negative, complaining people.

TRY THANK YOU THERAPY

I am thankful for . . .

- the taxes I pay . . . because it means I'm employed.
- the clothes that fit a little too snug . . . because it means I have enough to eat.
- my shadow who watches me work . . . because it means I am out in the sunshine.
- a lawn that needs mowing, windows that need cleaning and gutters that need fixing . . . because it means I have a home.
- the spot I find at the far end of the parking lot . . . because it means I am capable of walking.

- all the complaining I hear about our government . . . because it means we have freedom of speech.
- the lady behind me in church who sings off key . . . because it means I can hear.
- the piles of laundry and ironing . . . because if means my loved ones are nearby.
- the alarm that goes off in the early morning hours . . . because it means that I'm alive.
- weariness and aching muscles at the end of the day . . . because it means I have been productive.[3]

8. Write thank-you notes as a way of life.

The thank-you note is one of the most important things you can do when someone has done something for you. It shows that you are grateful and are not taking for granted anything done for you by someone else.

9. Identify people who have made a difference in your life and let them know it.

Think back about those who have contributed positively to your life. There have been several, perhaps many, along the way. It will bless you and them to let them know it. Don't wait until the funeral to send flowers. Do something now to say, "Thank you for what you have done for me."

10. Always be doing things for other people.

Lose yourself in helping others. Be so thankful for what God has done for you that you share your gratefulness with others. Live your life in an attempt to show God just how thankful you are for his blessings in your life.

THE HABIT OF
FAITH

11

POINT PASSAGE

And looking at them Jesus said to them, "With people this is impossible, but with God all things are possible."
MATTHEW 19:26

The Jesus habit of faith is choosing to trust God and believing what he said in his Word, no matter what you are facing.

> Faith does not ask for any other evidence than for the written Word of God.
> —Unknown

Jesus Showed Us How to Have Faith

Jesus implicitly trusted the Father in every situation at all times. He demonstrated total dependence on him even when the circumstances made no sense. He didn't have to see it to believe it. He believed the Father, and the Father always kept his word.

Jesus, in the garden of Gethsemane, trusted totally in the Father's will, although it grieved him.

> Then Jesus came with them to a place called Gethsemane, and said to His disciples, "Sit here while I go over there and pray." And He took with Him Peter and the two sons of Zebedee, and began to be grieved and distressed. Then He said to them, "My soul is deeply grieved, to the point of death; remain here and keep watch with Me." And He went a little beyond them, and fell on His face and prayed, saying, "My Father, if it is possible, let this cup pass from Me; yet not as I will, but

as You will." . . . He went away again a second time and
prayed, saying, "My Father, if this cannot pass away unless
I drink it, Your will be done." (Matt. 26:36–39, 42)

He conceded that whatever God
wanted was the very best. Faith accepts
God's plan as the best and doesn't seek
another way. Faith embraces God's will
even when it is not explainable at the
moment.

> You honor Jesus when
> you act in faith on His
> Word. —Ed Cole

Jesus exercised the greatest faith ever on the cross.

And Jesus, crying out with a loud voice, said,
"Father, INTO THY HANDS I COMMIT MY SPIRIT." (Luke
23:46)

Jesus took all he had done, all his suffering, and placed it in
the Father's hands—trusting him that his plan had been fulfilled.
Jesus may not have seen everything at the moment, but he trusted
God that his plan was accomplished. True faith simply looks to
God, not past God, trying to figure things out.

Jesus believed God could do the impossible.

And looking at them Jesus said to them, "With
people this is impossible, but with God all things are
possible." (Matt. 19:26)

F.A.I.T.H.

You have heard the acrostic
of FAITH—Forsaking All I Trust
Him. I have added a few more
that help us understand the
meaning of faith:

- Forget About Impossible
  Things and Hope.

- Father's Ability Invariably To
  Handle it.
- Forging Ahead I Trust Him.
- Fear Aside I Take Him.
- Finding Assurance In Times
  of Hardship.

Jesus' faith declared that there was nothing God couldn't do. Real faith says the same, "God can do anything, anywhere, at anytime."

> **Regret looks back.**
> **Worry looks around.**
> **Faith looks up.**
> **—John Mason**

Jesus had faith that the Father would raise him from the dead.

"Behold, we are going up to Jerusalem; and the Son of Man will be delivered to the chief priests and scribes, and they will condemn Him to death, and will hand Him over to the Gentiles to mock and scourge and crucify Him, and on the third day He will be raised up." (Matt. 20:18–19)

GET IN THE WHEELBARROW

There was a tightrope walker who did incredible aerial feats. All over Paris he would do tightrope acts at tremendously scary heights. Then he had succeeding acts: he would do it blindfolded; then he would go across the tightrope blindfolded, pushing a wheelbarrow. An American promoter read about this in the papers and wrote a letter to the tightrope walker, saying, "Tightrope, I don't believe you can do it, but I'm willing to make you an offer. For a very substantial sum of money, besides all your transportation fees, I would like to challenge you to do your act over Niagara Falls." Tightrope wrote back, "Sir, although I've never been to America and seen the Falls, I'd love to come." Well, after a lot of promotion and setting the whole thing up, many people came to see the event. Tightrope was to start on the Canadian side and come to the American side. Drums roll, and he comes across the rope, which is suspended over the treacherous part of the falls, blindfolded!! And he makes it across easily.

The crowds go wild, and he comes to the promoter and says, "Well, Mr. Promoter, now do you believe I can do it?" "Well of course I do. I mean, I just saw you do it." "No," said Tightrope, "do you really believe I can do it?" "Well of course I do, you just did it." "No, no, no," said Tightrope, "do you believe I can do it?" "Yes," said Mr. Promoter, "I believe you can do it." "Good," said Tightrope, "then you get in the wheelbarrow."[1]

Jesus fully expected God to raise him from the dead, just as he promised. Faith believes that the grave is not the end, that there is a coming resurrection.

> **Removing all risks from your life renders faith unnecessary. Faith requires risks.**
> **—Ken Mayhanes**

Jesus had faith that the Father always heard and answered his prayers.

So they removed the stone. Then Jesus raised His eyes, and said, "Father, I thank You that You have heard Me. I knew that You always hear Me; but because of the people standing around I said it, so that they may believe that You sent Me." (John 11:41–42)

Jesus never doubted that God would answer his prayers. That's the only way our prayers are answered. When there is doubt—lack of faith—that our prayers will be answered, it blocks what God wants to do.

But he must ask in faith without any doubting, for the one who doubts is like the surf of the sea, driven and tossed by the wind. For that man ought not to expect that he will receive anything from the Lord. (James 1:6–7)

This is the confidence which we have before Him, that, if we ask anything according to His will, He hears us. And if we know that He hears us in whatever we ask, we know that we have the requests which we have asked from Him. (1 John 5:14–15)

GOD'S HANDS ARE BIGGER

"A young boy went to the local store with his mother. The shop owner, a kindly man, passed him a large jar of suckers and invited him to help himself to a handful. The boy held back. So the shop owner pulled out a handful for him. When outside, the boy's mother asked why he had suddenly been so shy and wouldn't take a handful of suckers when offered. The boy replied, "Because his hand is much bigger than mine!"[2]

What Are the Enemies of the Habit of Faith?

1. Unbelief—I can't accept God's Word about it. I just don't think it could happen. I've got to see it to believe it.
2. Feeling—I just don't feel it.
3. People—That's not what he said. That's not what she said. According to the experts, that can't happen.
4. Lack of awareness—I'm not sure what the Bible says about that.

> True faith rests upon the character of God and asks no further proof than the moral perfections of the One who cannot lie. It is enough that God has said it. —A. W. Tozer

---

WHERE'S YOUR UMBRELLA?

Television interviewer and journalist Larry King describes three farmers who gather daily in a field during a horrible drought. The men are down on their knees, looking upward, and praying the skies will open and pour forth a much-needed rain. Unfortunately, the heavens are silent, and the petitioners become discouraged, but they continue to meet every morning to lift up their request to God. One morning an uninvited stranger approaches and asks the men what they are doing. They respond, "We're praying for rain." The newcomer looks at each of them and shakes his head, "No, I don't think so." The first farmer says, "Of course we're praying. We are down on our knees pleading for rain. Look around; see the drought. We haven't had rain in more than a year!" The outsider continues to nod his head and advises them their efforts will never work. The second farmer jumps in and says, "We need the rain; we aren't asking only for ourselves, but for our families and livestock."

The man listens, nods, and says he still isn't impressed. "You're wasting your time," he says. The third farmer can't take any more, and in anger he says, "OK, what would you do if you were in our shoes?" The visitor asks, "You really want to know?" The three landowners answer, "We really want to know! The future of our farmlands is at stake." The guest announces, "I would have brought an umbrella!"[3]

Make Faith a Habit

1. Faith, like muscles, is developed.

> Faith is: dead to doubts, dumb to discouragements, blind to impossibilities.
> —**Unknown**

It is developed through trusting God's Word over time. Faith must be exercised in everyday situations in order for it to grow. There are multiple opportunities for you to flex your faith muscles. The more you use them, the stronger they will become.

2. Find what God says about it.

Whatever the issue, get God's Word on it. Underline it. Circle it. Hang onto it. Remind God of it. God's Word forms the basis for your faith. It is the platform on which faith stands. Stand on God's promises.

3. Forget about your feelings.

Feelings and faith are not on the same team. They often face off in the arena of life, and the strongest one wins. For faith to win, feelings must not have the last word.

4. Be content to let God know some things you don't.

It's OK not to know some things. There are things that only God knows. We can't explain it, and it doesn't seem logical, but you choose to believe God anyway. We don't have to understand it, only trust in a sovereign God that he knows what is best and he is still in control.

5. Understand that God is . . .

- All-powerful—He can do anything and everything.
- All-present—He is always everywhere at the same time and is right at the point of your need.
- All-knowing—He knows everything about the past, present, and future, and he knows exactly what you need, when you need it, and where you need it.

6. Compare what others are saying and what your circumstances are saying with what God has said in his Word.

Choose to believe his Word. At times it may mean going against popular opinion and even standing alone. God's Word will still be standing long after people and circumstances have passed.

7. Wait on God.

There may be a testing time before the answer comes in order to strengthen your faith. An untested faith is a weak faith. You can count on your faith being the target of multiple trials. If your faith is never tested, it will never grow.

> Attempt something so impossible that unless God is in it, it's doomed to failure.
> —John Haggai

7. Realize that there is no other way you can please God apart from faith.

"Without faith it is impossible to please [God]." (Heb. 11:6) God has chosen faith as the way for you to bless him and him to bless you. Take out faith, and you take away your ability to please God.

8. Try something so big that unless God is in it, it is destined to fail.

This has often been called a "God thing," something that only God could have pulled off. "Attempt great things for God, expect great things from God" is the response of a person of faith.

9. Don't mix faith with presumption—presuming upon God to do something that is not within his sovereign will.

Faith's boundaries are in the will of God found within the Word of God. It is testing God when we assume he will do something that runs contrary to "thus saith the Lord."

THE HABIT OF
MOTIVATION

12

POINT PASSAGE

*"For I gave you an example that
you also should do as I did to you."*
JOHN 13:15

The Jesus habit of motivation is using everything you have and, by example, encouraging other people to be their best and do their best.

> Motivation is what gets
> you started. Habit is
> what keeps you going.
> —Jim Ryan

Jesus Showed Us How to Motivate

Jesus was the preeminent motivator. He said things, did things, set up things to encourage people to go beyond, reach higher, and do more than they ever dreamed possible. Like a coach he showed people that they could live life on the highest level. He knew how to help people get from ordinary to extraordinary and from natural to supernatural. He motivated people not only by his words but by his example.

Jesus showed us how to motivate people. Listen to these examples taken from actual words he shared with people.

Go.

Jesus said to him, "If you wish to be complete, go and sell your possessions and give to the poor, and you will have treasure in heaven; and come, follow Me." (Matt. 19:21)

"Go therefore and make disciples of all the nations, baptizing them in the name of the Father and the Son and the Holy Spirit." (Matt. 28:19)

Get up.

And Jesus came to them and touched them and said, "Get up, and do not be afraid." (Matt. 17:7)

Jesus said to him, "Get up, pick up your pallet and walk." (John 5:8)

"Which is easier, to say, 'Your sins have been forgiven you,' or to say, 'Get up and walk'?" (Luke 5:23)

Believe.

"Do not let your heart be troubled; believe in God, believe also in Me." (John 14:1)

Ask, seek, knock.

"If you ask Me anything in My name, I will do it." (John 14:14)

BRINGING GOD TO WORK

According to *USA Today*, firms are spending billions of dollars to fire up workers—with little results. The article states: There has been exhaustive academic research trying to find out what motivates workers, and it has turned up almost no evidence that motivational spending makes any difference. Poll-taker Gallup analyzed its massive database and determined in March [2001] that 55 percent of employees have no enthusiasm for their work—Gallup uses the term "not engaged"—based on several criteria, including loyalty and the desire to improve job performance. One in five (19 percent) are so uninterested or negative about their jobs that they poison the workplace to the point that companies might be better off if they called in sick. Further into the article, Spencer Johnson, author of *Who Moved My Cheese?* states he "believes research may one day show that the only long-lasting motivation will come from employees who bring it to work in the form of God, spirituality, or something else that causes them to 'rise to a higher purpose.'"[1]

"Ask, and it will be given to you; seek, and you will find; knock, and it will be opened to you. For everyone who asks receives, and he who seeks finds, and to him who knocks it will be opened." (Matt. 7:7–8)

> There is only one way under high heaven to get anybody to do anything. Did you ever stop to think of that? Yes, just one way. And that is by making the other person want to do it. —Dale Carnegie

Take up your cross, deny yourself, and follow Jesus.

And He was saying to them all, "If anyone wishes to come after Me, he must deny himself, and take up his cross daily and follow Me." (Luke 9:23)

Come.

"Come to Me, all who are weary and heavy-laden, and I will give you rest." (Matt. 11:28)

And He said, "Come!" And Peter got out of the boat, and walked on the water and came toward Jesus. (Matt. 14:29)

Be of good cheer.

"These things I have spoken unto you, that in me ye might have peace. In the world ye shall have tribulation: but be of good cheer; I have overcome the world." (John 16:33 KJV)

Repent.

And saying, "The time is fulfilled, and the kingdom of God is at hand; repent and believe in the gospel." (Mark 1:15)

With God all things are possible.

And looking at them Jesus said to them, "With people this is impossible, but with God all things are possible." (Matt. 19:26)

What Are the Enemies of the Habit of Motivation?

1.   Laziness—I can't even motivate myself; how can I motivate others?

2.   Indifference—So what?

3.   Comfort—I just don't want to change.

Make Motivation a Habit

1. Find your motivation in Christ by daily being in his Word and being in his will.

There is no motivation like the motivation that comes from daily encountering God through the discipline of Bible study and prayer. It gives you the necessary "umph" to keep going.

2. Believe that you have the power, through Christ, to change the world.

It is taking seriously Paul's statement, "I can do all things through [Christ] who strengthens me" (Phil. 4:13). It is not because of any strength on our own, but the power that comes through an empty grave. Living in the reality of the power of the resurrection gives us confidence that things can change.

3. Live a life that motivates people to go beyond where they are.

Set the example. Be a living demonstration that people can be more and do more than is expected. Like the apostle Paul, we should be able to say, "Do as I do." Those who say it can't be done should never stand in the way of those who are doing it.

4. Be positive and proactive.

Let your words be motivators for people to reach higher. Words are the most powerful instruments in the world. Our

> Seventy psychologists were asked, 'What is the most essential thing for a supervisor to know about human nature?' Two-thirds said that 'motivation and an understanding of what makes people think, feel, and act as they do' is uppermost.
> —Roy Zuck[2]

words can be a force for God and for good. Solomon tells us that life and death are in the power of the tongue. Use life-giving, hope-filling words to motivate people to live life to the max.

5. Believe that all things are possible through God.

This concept must be imbedded in our central belief system. It is the "God can" philosophy of life. There is no such thing as an impossibility to God. Nothing is too hard for him, and no situation catches him by surprise.

6. Dare to dream big and communicate that dream, inviting others to be a part of it.

Our lives should always have in them something God sized, something that is so big that only God could do it. I keep a prayer list with me labeled, "The Ten Impossible Things I Am Asking God to Do." It keeps me thinking in terms of something bigger than myself.

HERE TO FINISH

During the Olympic marathon race in 1968, the world saw a clear picture of true commitment. John Akhwari was running for Tanzania, and although he didn't win the race, he won the hearts of all who saw him run. Akhwari was injured by a fall early in the race. Most runners would have conceded defeat and dropped out of the race to receive proper medical attention, but on this cool night in Mexico City, John Akhwari picked himself up and quickly bandaged his bleeding leg. The injury took its toll, but this determined Tanzanian wasn't going to quit. He kept running, even though he was miles behind the main pack. Finally, more than an hour after all of the other runners had finished, John Akhwari limped into the stadium that was now almost completely empty of spectators. Slowly he jogged the final lap and crossed the finish line in virtual solitude. Bud Greenspan, a respected commentator, watched the spectacle from a distance. He was so intrigued by the heroic finish that he walked over to this physically depleted young man and asked why he continued the race after sustaining such an injury. John Akhwari replied, "My country did not send me nine thousand miles to start the race. They sent me to finish the race."[3]

7. Surround yourself with can-do people.

Don't hang around negative people. You will discover that you take on the attitudes of the people with whom you spend the most time. Negative people will drag you down, while positive, proactive people will lift you up.

8. Remember failure is the greatest teacher.

When you fail, make friends with that failure. We learn lessons in failure that we can get nowhere else. History is filled with lessons of how the greatest blessings and results have been born out of the ashes of failure. Future success depends on the response of the person to failure.

9. Don't accept the response of, "That's just the way things are."

That statement is resplendent with a defeatist attitude. I call it a "concession mentality"—simply conceding that nothing can be done to change the situation.

10. Focus on those who are most likely to be motivated.

Be wise with your time. Many desire to be motivated. They want to go beyond where they are, they simply need someone to encourage them. Some people simply don't desire to be motivated. We should spend little time attempting to motivate those who have no desire to be more and do more than what they are presently doing.

THE HABIT OF
HANDLING
CRITICISM
EFFECTIVELY

POINT PASSAGE

"No one was able to answer Him a word, nor did anyone dare from that day on to ask Him another question."
MATTHEW 22:46

The Jesus habit of handling criticism effectively is choosing to respond to criticism with love, truth, and humility, and sometimes with no visible response at all, thus demonstrating the love of God and allowing him to be your defense.

> If one man calls you a horse, ignore him; if two men call you a horse, consider it; if three men call you a horse, buy a saddle.
> —Persian proverb

Jesus Showed Us How to Handle Criticism Effectively

Jesus was often on the receiving end of criticism, yet he always handled it effectively. It certainly must have hurt, but he never allowed criticism to debilitate or stop him. He was especially criticized by the religious leaders. Unfortunately, religious people can be the most critical. Even while on the cross, Jesus was subjected to criticism by the soldiers, the crowds, and one of the thieves on the cross beside him.

Anyone who attempts big things, great things, God-sized things; who makes big plans, sets majestic goals, steps out in faith, and dares to take a risk will be criticized.

Jesus was criticized because the religious leaders were jealous of him and felt threatened by his popularity.

Then a demon-possessed man who was blind and mute was brought to Jesus, and He healed him, so that the mute man spoke and saw. All the crowds were amazed, and were saying, "This man cannot be the Son of David, can he?" But when the Pharisees heard this, they said, "This man casts out demons only by Beelzebul the ruler of the demons." (Matt. 12:22–24)

Jesus was real. He genuinely performed miracles from God. The religious leaders allowed their jealousy to speak in the form of criticism. Sometimes what people can't understand, they criticize. People who are jealous often manifest it by being critical.

Jesus was criticized for his faith.

Now the chief priests and the whole Council kept trying to obtain false testimony against Jesus, so that

---

WHO'S JOHNNY CARSON?

Whether you like Jay Leno, Johnny Carson, or *The Tonight Show,* an interesting lesson can be found from NBC's late-night studio. When Leno became the new host of *The Tonight Show,* he took some real heat. Critics unfavorably compared him to his predecessor, Johnny Carson. From all of the criticism you would have thought he was in big trouble, but he never got too worried. In fact, he kept a stack of unpleasant reviews on his desk for inspiration. One critic said, "Too many soft questions." Another one read, "He's being too nice." These unkind words didn't bother Leno, though, because they were written in 1962 and were directed at Jack Paar's replacement, "an awkward nobody named Johnny Carson." Few people succeed without criticism.[1]

they might put Him to death. They did not find any, even though many false witnesses came forward. But later on two came forward, and said, "This man stated, 'I am able to destroy the temple of God and to rebuild it in three days.'" The high priest stood up and said to Him, "Do You not answer? What is it that

> If people speak ill of you, live so that no one will believe them.
> —Plato

these men are testifying against You?" But Jesus kept silent. And the high priest said to Him, "I adjure You by the living God, that You tell us whether You are the Christ, the Son of God." (Matt. 26:59–63)

Jesus' faith in God and his belief in God's Word that he would die and be raised to life the third day caused the religious leaders to criticize him. Sometimes we are criticized at work, at school, among peers, or for our faith. We are certainly no better than Jesus.

Jesus sometimes responded to criticism by remaining silent.

But Jesus kept silent. And the high priest said to Him, "I adjure You by the living God, that You tell us whether You are the Christ, the Son of God." (Matt. 26:63)

Now Jesus stood before the governor, and the governor questioned Him, saying, "Are You the King of the Jews?" And Jesus said to him, "It is as you say." And while He was being accused by the chief priests and elders, He did not answer. (Matt. 27:11–12)

Jesus' silence meant he would not even acknowledge the criticism as worthy of an answer. Silence is the best response to criticism in some situations.

Jesus, at times, considered the source of the criticism and dismissed it.

Then Pilate said to Him, "Do You not hear how many things they testify against You?" And He did not answer him with regard to even a single charge, so that the governor was quite amazed." (Matt. 27:13–14)

Some people are perennially critical. The only right response is to dismiss their criticism.

Jesus, at appropriate times, addressed the criticism and set the record straight.

Then the Pharisees went and plotted together how they might trap Him in what He said. And they sent their disciples to Him, along with the Herodians, saying, "Teacher, we know that You are truthful and teach the way of God in truth, and defer to no one; for You are not partial to any. Tell us then, what do You think? Is it lawful to give a poll-tax to Caesar, or not?" But Jesus perceived their malice, and said, "Why are you testing Me, you hypocrites? Show Me the coin used for the poll-tax." And they brought Him a denarius. And He said to them, "Whose likeness and inscription is this?" They said to Him, "Caesar's." Then He said to them, "Then render to Caesar the things that are Caesar's; and to God the things that are God's." And hearing this, they were amazed, and leaving Him, they went away. (Matt. 22:15–22)

> At a press conference, Billy Graham was criticized. He got up and said, "Let's pray. Oh Lord, please help us to never be guilty of that which our critics are saying about us."
> —T. W. Wilson[2]

The Pharisees thought they had Jesus in a trap concerning the question of paying taxes. His answer silenced them. There are times when we need to speak up, take a stand, share the facts, and squelch a rumor.

What Are the Enemies of the Habit of Handling Criticism Effectively?

1. Defensiveness—I'm not going to let you get by with this.
2. Anger—You are really upsetting me.

3. Pride—How dare you question me!
4. Revenge—I'll get you back.
5. Bitterness—I will not forgive.

Make Handling Criticism Effectively a Habit

1. Expect criticism if you dare to attempt anything for God and for good.

It is not if, but when, because criticism will come your way when you follow God. Don't be surprised when someone says something or does something to let you know he or she doesn't approve of your commitment to God.

A BIG MOUTH SILENCED

Let me share with you about Precesso Marcellos, a Filipino, who never finished high school when he received Christ into his life. He later became an evangelist and has had a radio program for years. Listen to how this man added Jesus to a situation.

He was asked to conduct the funeral of a well-known pastor in the Philippines. A known critic of Christianity was in the audience. As Precesso was preaching, the critic stood up in the middle of his funeral sermon and says, "I have a question."

He was told, "I'm in the middle of my message. Let me finish my message, and then I will answer your question."

At the conclusion he said to the man, "Now what is your question?"

"Your Jesus says you will do greater works than he did. What greater works have you done?"

Precesso responded, "Well,

Jesus was only able to preach to a few thousand or so, but on the radio I am able to preach to millions."

The critic said, "No, that's not what I mean. Can you raise the dead like Jesus? If you can do greater works, then raise this man in the casket from the dead."

He responded, "Jesus chose whom he raised from the dead. He didn't just go around and raise everyone."

The critic continued, "Then whom do you choose to raise from the dead?"

Precesso thought. "I choose you. Please kill yourself, then I will raise you from the dead. If I raise you from the dead, then I'm right, but if I can't, then you're right."

The people roared with laughter and the critic was silenced.

---

2. Consider the source.

You may need to say, "There he goes again." Some people live in a critical condition. You simply know when you encounter them that they are probably going to say something critical or negative. Rather than receive what they say, dismiss the criticism based on the critic.

3. Attend "criticism university."

Learn all you can through the criticism. Ask, "Is there any truth to it?" If so, apologize, make it right. In every criticism there may be a morsel of truth that can help you become better. Squeeze every nugget of knowledge from the criticism. Don't hesitate to apologize when the criticism is true. It is much easier to admit when you are wrong than to try to defend it.

> "When attacked by a dragon, do not become one."
>
> —Marshall Shelley[3]

4. Let the person finish.

Don't interrupt. This can be difficult since our first response is immediately to defend ourselves. Hear the person through. Let the person talk. The more people talk the more you can learn. Listening gives you an opportunity to earn the right to respond when they finish.

5. Ask the person to pray for you and help you.

Be genuine in this. Seek the person's prayer. Ask the person to take this area of concern and take it daily to the Lord in prayer on your behalf. Don't be so prideful that you let the opportunity pass you by to receive a blessing from another person's constructive criticism. We can always improve.

6. You may need to remain silent and then simply thank the person.

Saying nothing may be your best option, depending on the situation. Smile, don't smirk at the person. Be kind and gentle and say, "Thank you," and simply let that be it.

7. If someone has criticized you and the criticism is damaging your character, share the truth in love, but don't attack the critic.

Separate the criticism from the critic. Go after the criticism if it is damaging your credibility. In love, confront the criticism with the truth and then leave it in God's hands.

8. Pray for your critics.

Write their names down on a list and pray for them every day. It's difficult to be bitter toward someone you are constantly making the target of your prayers. Ask God to bless your critics and to give them wisdom to see the truth and accept it.

9. Trust that if you are right, time and truth are your best friends.

If you do the right thing, eventually it will come out. Truth is vindicated over time. Let God defend you. You will be amazed at those who discover later that what you said and what you did were the right responses.

10. Do something nice for your critics.

This will help you not to hold onto a grudge. Go out of your way to express kindness to the person. Make it a priority to show your critics the love of Jesus in practical ways.

THE HABIT OF
FAMILY PRIORITY

POINT PASSAGE

*"Is not this the carpenter's son? Is not His mother
called Mary, and His brothers, James and Joseph and Simon
and Judas? And His sisters, are they not all with us? Where
then did this man get all these things?"*
MATTHEW 13:55–56

The Jesus habit of family priority is choosing consistently to put your family and their needs ahead of your own, others, work, recreation, or anything else.

> A family is a place where principles are hammered and honed on the anvil of everyday living.
> —Charles Swindoll

Jesus Showed Us How to Have Family Priority

Jesus demonstrated his commitment to family. As man, he had an earthly family; as God, he was creating a spiritual family where, because of his sacrifice, we could come to know a common Father.

"For the Son of Man has come to seek and to save that which was lost." (Luke 19:10)

The purpose of this study, however, is to focus on his earthly family and how he related to them.

Jesus honored his family.

"Is not this the carpenter's son? Is not His mother called Mary, and His brothers, James and Joseph and Simon and Judas? And His sisters, are they not all with us? Where then did this man get all these things?" (Matt. 13:55–56)

We see Jesus obeying his mother Mary, and stepfather, Joseph. He loved His siblings. He honored His stepfather, Joseph, by working with him for thirty years in the family business, a carpenter shop. Jesus was keeping the fifth commandment.

> People committed to their family as the number one priority in their lives become more successful across the board.
> —Derk Maul

> "Honor your father and your mother, that your days may be prolonged in the land which the LORD your God gives you." (Exod. 20:12)

His life, death, and resurrection had an obvious impact on his half brothers James and Jude. Both wrote books of the Bible and became leaders in the early New Testament church.

Your family is your greatest place of influence. How you relate to your family defines the impact of your Christianity.

Jesus identified with his family.

His family was a humble one. They were not wealthy or prestigious. The town where Jesus was raised, Nazareth, wasn't known for anything significant. Yet he loved them and identified with them.

How Much Is an Hour of Your Time?

A father came home tired and irritable. His son asked his father how much money he made in an hour. The father, not in a good mood, answered harshly, "I make $20 an hour." A little later the son asked his father if he would give him $10. By now the father was really agitated and gave him the brush off. Later that evening the father felt he had been harsh and went to his son's room and gave him the ten dollars. The son reached under his pillow and pulled out some crumpled dollar bills. Now the father blew up and asked why he asked for more money when he already had some. The boy said, "I did not have enough but I do now. Daddy, can I buy an hour of your time?"[1]

> "Is not this the carpenter, the son of Mary, and
> brother of James and Joses and Judas and Simon? Are
> not His sisters here with us?" And they took offense at
> Him. (Mark 6:3)

Don't deny your family. God gave them to you for a reason.
It may even be a dysfunctional family, but God can use them and
use you in their lives.

One of Jesus' last acts on the cross, before he died, was to show his love and care for his mother

> When Jesus then saw His mother, and the disciple
> whom He loved standing nearby, He said to His mother,
> "Woman, behold, your son!" Then He said to the disci-
> ple, "Behold, your mother!" From that hour the disciple
> took her into his own household. (John 19:26–27)

The sin of the world was all put on Jesus. Eternity hung in the
balance. Nails were in his hands and feet. He had been beaten
beyond recognition. He was bleeding profusely. The sin of the
world on him had separated him from the Father. He was lonely.
He hurt as no one has ever hurt. Yet he looked at John and said,
"Take care of my mother. Take her into your home and treat her as
your own mother."

THIS IS NOT YOUR GRANDFATHER'S FAMILY

The US Census Bureau has come out with several findings in regard to the American family in the 1990s: Households headed by unmarried partners grew by almost 72 percent during the decade. Households headed by single mothers or fathers increased by 25 percent and 62 percent, respectively. And for the first time ever, nuclear families dropped below 25 percent of all households. Thirty-three percent of all babies were born to unmarried women, compared to only 3.8 percent in 1940. Cohabitation increased by close to 1,000 percent from 1960 to 1998.[2]

What Are the Enemies of the Habit of Family Priority?

1. Time—One of these days I will . . . .
2. Work—I've got to make a living.
3. Selfishness—What about my needs?

Make Family Priority a Habit

1. Recognize that according to God, the greatest priority on earth is your family.

That is God's order of priority. The family God has given to you must become your first priority, after your relationship with Jesus Christ. The family is the first institution God established.

2. In God's order of priority your marriage comes first, then your children.

> The family is the most basic unit of government. As the first community to which a person is attached and the first authority under which a person learns to live, the family establishes society's most basic values.
> —Charles Colson

It is a great mistake for parents to put their children before their marriage partners. When meeting the needs of one's marriage partner becomes the priority, parenting is strengthened. A strong marriage is the family's greatest ally.

3. Admit that you cannot do this without God's power.

To be the marriage partner and parent you need to be requires God's intervention in your life. As wonderful as marriage and parenting can be, they can be the most challenging assignments we will ever be presented. With God's help, our family can be our greatest life experience.

4. Calendar family time.

If it is not calendared, it probably won't happen. We calendar nearly every other event in our lives yet often fail specifically to incorporate into our schedules that which is most important. Each week have a planned-out family time. Quantity time, not just quality time, is essential.

5. Be Jesus to your family—serving them.

This especially applies to fathers, whom God has placed as spiritual leaders in the home. Each family member should see himself or herself as representing Jesus to his or her family. Remember, Jesus came to serve, not be served.

> As the family goes, so goes the nation and so goes the whole world in which we live.
> —**Pope John Paul II**

6. Eat at least one meal together every day and pray together at that time.

Our society has gotten away from this, and the effects are negative. The meal is a time of sharing, fellowship, listening, laughing, asking questions, and getting reacquainted with one another. It is the one time when everyone can be together. After you eat, spend time sitting there and talking with one another. Sacrifices will have to be made to make this happen, but the rewards are worth it.

IF YOU WANT A STRONG FAMILY

From a national survey of strong families conducted by the Human Development and Family Department at the University of Nebraska-Lincoln, a profile of a strong family:

Appreciation. Family members gave one another compliments and sincere demonstrations of approval. They tried to make the others feel appreciated and good about themselves.

Ability to deal with crises in a positive manner. They were willing to take a bad situation, see something positive in it and focus on that.

Time together. In all areas of their lives—meals, work, recreation—they structured their schedules to spend time together.

High degree of commitment. Families promoted each person's happiness and welfare, invested time and energy in one another and made family their number one priority.

Good communication patterns. These families spent time talking with one another. They also listened well, which shows respect.

High degree of religious orientation. Not all belonged to an organized church, but they considered themselves highly religious.[3]

7. If your job is damaging your family, either adjust your schedule or change jobs.

Your family must take precedence over your job. Now there are exceptional times when you have to make a sacrifice for work. No one ever comes to the end of his life and says, "I wish I had spent more time at work." Many, however, regret that they didn't spend more time with their family.

8. Listen to your family.

Every family member should have a voice. Whether it is a parent or a child, each should listen attentively to the other. Become approachable to your family, giving them the freedom to share how they feel.

> It is my view that our society can be no more stable than the foundation of individual family units upon which it rests. Our government, our institutions, our schools, indeed, our way of life are dependent on healthy marriages and loyalty to the vulnerable little children around our feet.
> —James Dobson, Focus on the Family

9. Have fun together.

Laugh together. Let there be laughter in the walls of your home. Your family should be able to look back and remember the funny things that happened. Deliberately create fun moments within your home. Humor is a great family asset.

10. Be principle centered, based on the Bible, not rules-driven.

The biggest difference between the two is the attitude in which they are presented. Rules-driven homes can be cold and legalistic, placing the rule ahead of the person. To be sure, there must be rules, but rules based on biblical principles will bring out the best in people.

11. Consistently go to church together.

Worshipping together consistently in church greatly strengthens marriage and family relationships. Hit-and-miss church attendance, as well as not having a church home, hinders the effect that consistent attendance at the same church offers.

THE HABIT OF
OBEDIENCE

POINT PASSAGE

*"If you keep My commandments, you will abide in
My love; just as I have kept My Father's commandments
and abide in His love."*

JOHN 15:10

The Jesus habit of obedience is choosing to act on God's will, based on what he has said in his Word and following the leading of the Holy Spirit where there is no clear word in Scripture about what to do.

> You can never go wrong when you choose to obey Christ.
> —Unknown

Jesus Showed Us How to be Obedient

Jesus always, in every circumstance, obeyed the Father. His life was a yes to his will. Jesus' impact was the result of his total and instant obedience. Our salvation depended on Jesus' obedience.

Jesus had many opportunities to by pass the Father's will, but he didn't.

Then Jesus was led up by the Spirit into the wilderness to be tempted by the devil. And after He had fasted forty days and forty nights, He then became hungry. And the tempter came and said to Him, "If You are the Son of God, command that these stones become bread." But He answered and said, "It is written, 'Man shall not live on bread alone, but on every word that proceeds out of the mouth of God.'"

Then the devil took Him into the holy city and had Him stand on the pinnacle of the temple, and said to Him, "If You are the Son of God, throw Yourself down; for it is written, 'He will command His angels concerning

---

NO CHICKEN ON SUNDAYS

Doing Business God's Way—Truett Cathy has answered the question, What would Jesus do? The founder of Chick-fil-A restaurants is a successful businessman, but for many, he is even better known—and respected—for letting his faith guide his business operation. Here are a few examples:

Mr. Cathy's restaurants have been closed on Sundays since 1948. The seventy-nine-year-old CEO of the nearly one thousand Chick-fil-A restaurants doesn't mind losing millions of dollars of business to honor the Lord's Day.

At his first restaurant in 1948, he hired a Eddie J. White, a twelve-year-old African-American. This was an unpopular choice during a time of segregation. He also mentored an orphan, Woody Faulk, since he was thirteen. Today Woody is vice president of product development of Chick-fil-A.

Cathy developed a successful foster home system called WinShape Homes. There are now eleven homes in the US and one in Brazil. His daughter Trudy and son-in-law John were Southern Baptist missionaries at the Brazil home for ten years. His Camp WinShape and the WinShape Foundation provide scholarships for kids and college students.

One of his favorite truisms is, "It's easier to build boys and girls than to mend men and women." Chick-fil-A Kids Meals don't come with promotional toys from the latest popular movie. Instead he offers VeggieTales books, audiocassettes of Focus on the Family's Adventures in Odyssey, and other character-building materials. Woody Faulk gives a good summary of Cathy's character: "A lot of people look on Truett as Santa Claus, but he's not. He'll meet you halfway so that you can learn a lesson from the process. He's the personification of James 1:22: 'Do not merely listen to the word, and so deceive yourselves. Do what it says.' (NIV). I sincerely owe my life to that man."[1]

You'; and 'On their hands they will bear You up, so that You will not strike Your foot against a stone.'" Jesus said to him, "On the other hand, it is written, 'You shall not put the Lord your God to the test.'"

Again, the devil took Him to a very high mountain and showed Him all the kingdoms of the world and their glory; and he said to Him, "All these things I will give You, if You fall down and worship me." Then Jesus said to him, "Go, Satan! For it is written, 'You shall worship the Lord Your God and serve Him only.'" Then the devil left Him; and behold, angels came and began to minister to Him. (Matt. 4:1–11)

> The cost of obedience is small compared with the cost of disobedience. —Unknown

Satan hit him hard with temptation offering him three opportunities to avoid the cross. Jesus fought to obey God. Obedience is not always easy. Satan will put up a fight. Our flesh will struggle.

From that time Jesus began to show His disciples that He must go to Jerusalem, and suffer many things from the elders and chief priests and scribes, and be killed, and be raised up on the third day. Peter took Him aside and began to rebuke Him, saying, "God forbid it, Lord! This shall never happen to You." But He turned and said to Peter, "Get behind Me, Satan! You are a stumbling block to Me; for you are not setting your mind on God's interests, but man's." (Matt. 16:21–23)

Even those Jesus was closest to attempted to get him to detour the way of the cross. Satan can use those who may have good intentions to prevent us from what the Father asks of us.

Jesus let us know that obedience has a cost

Saying, "Father, if You are willing, remove this cup from Me; yet not My will, but Yours be done." (Luke 22:42)

In the garden of Gethsemane, the Father showed Jesus the cost. Jesus still said, "Yes, I'll pay it." There is a price tag for obedience. It often requires that we lay our convenience and comfort on the altar.

Jesus' basis for obedience was the Scriptures

> After this, Jesus, knowing that all things had already been accomplished, to fulfill the Scripture, said, "I am thirsty." (John 19:28)

Jesus knew the Old Testament. He understood what God wanted him to do through the Scripture. Knowing God's Word gives us the insight into what God requires from us. Obedience is our right response to Scripture.

What Are the Enemies of the Habit of Obedience?

1. Flesh—I don't want to do that.
2. Satan—There's an easier way.
3. Procrastination—Let me think about it. Not now.
4. Convenience—There's too much to give up right now.
5. People—What will they think?

UPPER LIMIT PRICE

Following Christ Without Limits—I have vivid memories as a kid of my father taking me to an auction sale, telling me, "Don't scratch your nose at the wrong time, son." He said to me, "Always remember this: whenever you go to an auction sale, make sure you know your upper limit price."

That is ingrained in me. The great danger for us is that we walk into the Christian life knowing clearly our upper-limit price. Jesus does not allow us to set that. "If you save your life, you will lose it; but if you lose you life for my sake and the gospels, you will keep it," said Jesus [Mark 8:35].

Our calling is to a life of unconditional obedience where the price is unknown.[2]

Make Obedience a Habit

1. Choose obedience.

Obedience is always a choice. You don't have to feel like it to do it. There is no excuse for not doing the right thing. The option of obedience is always on the table. If we wait until we feel like it to obey God, obedience would probably never come. Like Nike, we "just do it!"

> The only part of the Bible you truly believe is the part you obey.
> —Unknown

2. Accept that the feeling of having obeyed God is the greatest feeling you will ever experience.

It is a much greater feeling than the short-lived pleasure of saying yes to temptation. We can't live on feelings, but feelings are important. There is no greater high than when you have obeyed God and said no to Satan's attempt to lead you out of the will of God.

3. Understand that your happiness in life depends upon your saying yes to God.

As we do what God said, the immediate result is an inner joy. A Christian who has stepped out of the will of God is not a happy Christian. If you are not happy, the first thing to ask is, "Have I failed to obey God?"

4. List things in Scripture that clearly show are God's will for your life.

Saying yes to those things clearly revealed as God's will in the Bible allows more light to shine on those specific things God wants for your life that are not recorded in Scripture. You can't expect light for the next step until you obey the light God has clearly given, those specific commands in Scripture.

5. Recognize that when you obey God, his power is released.

The power of God for our lives is tied to our obedience. The point of obedience becomes God's target for power.

6. For matters not clearly spelled out in Scripture, seek a scriptural principle and ask the Holy Spirit to give you either peace or a lack of peace about a particular decision.

The Holy Spirit, like an umpire, either will give you a peace or there will be a check in your spirit, a hesitancy that says, "Wait just a minute, something's not quite right." Principles in Scripture will always help us decide what to do.

7. Realize that when you become a Christian, you surrender your rights to do things your way.

Often we hear people say, "It's my life; I can do what I want to with it." The Christian cannot make that claim. Our body, mind, emotions, and will belong to him. We are not the captains of our own soul, the masters of our fate. God alone is our control.

8. Confess disobedience immediately and say yes to God's will.

When you know you have disobeyed God, stop what you are doing and make it right. Ask God to forgive you for not following his way. Thank God he is the God of a second chance. Start immediately doing what he told you to do.

9. Be aware that obedience brings the favor of God upon your life.

The favor of God is God's smile upon you. It is God's affirmation of your obedience. That favor creates an atmosphere where divine appointments and God's protection can take place in your life.

It is not difficult in our world to get a person interested in the message of the Gospel; it is terrifically difficult to sustain the interest. Millions of people in our culture make decisions for Christ, but there is a dreadful attrition rate. Many claim to have been born again, but the evidence for mature Christian discipleship is slim. In our kind of culture anything, even news about God, can be sold if it is packaged freshly; but when it loses its novelty, it goes on the garbage heap. There is a great market for religious experience in our world; there is little enthusiasm for the patient acquisition of virtue, little inclination to sign up for a long apprenticeship in what earlier Christians called holiness.
—Eugene Peterson[3]

10. Live in an environment where obedience is encouraged—church, Bible study, accountability group, personal quiet time, worship, reading Christian books.

Your environment will make all the difference in your desire to obey God. When you surround yourself with that which promotes saying yes to God, doing the right thing becomes more desirable.

THE HABIT OF
HONORING
THE GOVERNMENT

POINT PASSAGE

And He said to them, "Then render to Caesar the things that are Caesar's, and to God the things that are God's."

LUKE 20:25

The Jesus habit of honoring the government is choosing to see the government as a God-ordained institution that should be supported voluntarily through the obeying of its laws.

> It is the duty of all nations to acknowledge the providence of Almighty God, to obey his will, to be grateful for his benefits and humbly implore his protection and favor.
> —George Washington

Jesus Showed Us How to Honor the Government

Jesus was not antigovernment. He realized it was an institution that should be upheld, honored, and its laws obeyed. This does not mean he could not criticize the government if it ran counter to God's will. By working within the confines of the government, it allowed him the freedom to communicate his message.

Jesus paid taxes

He never sought to avoid paying taxes.

When they came to Capernaum, those who collected the two-drachma tax came to Peter and said, "Does your teacher not pay the two-drachma tax?" He said, "Yes." And when he came into the house, Jesus spoke to him first, saying, "What do you think, Simon? From whom do the kings of the earth collect customs or poll-tax, from their sons or from strangers?" When Peter said, "From strangers," Jesus said to him, "Then the sons are exempt. However, so that we do not offend them, go to the sea and throw in a hook, and take the first fish that comes up; and when you open its mouth, you will find a shekel. Take that and give it to them for you and Me." (Matt. 17:24–27)

Jesus believed in influencing the government through impacting the lives of leaders in government.

He influenced Matthew, a tax collector.

STILL "UNDER GOD"

"On Sunday, June 30, 2002, CNN reported that a weekend poll said nearly nine in ten Americans believe the phrase "under God" should remain in the pledge of allegiance. Most also believe that it is acceptable for the government to promote religious expression, as long as no specific religion is mentioned, according to a *Newsweek* poll.

"When asked if the pledge of allegiance should contain the phrase "under God," 87 percent of those polled by *Newsweek* said yes and only 9 percent said no. Asked if the government should avoid promoting religion in any way, 36 percent said yes, but 54 percent said no, and 60 percent of poll respondents said they think it is good for the country when government leaders pub-

licly express their faith in God.

"Only 12 percent of those polled thought the government should eliminate all references to God and religious belief in schools, government buildings, and other public settings, while 84 percent said such references are acceptable as long as they don't mention a specific religion.

"The poll found that 45 percent of Americans hold the view that the United States is a secular nation in which religious belief, or lack of it, isn't a defining characteristic. Twenty-nine percent believe the United States is a Christian nation, and another 16 percent believe the United States is a biblical nation, defined by the Judeo-Christian tradition."[1]

And as Jesus passed on from there, He saw a man, called Matthew, sitting in the tax office; and He said to him, "Follow Me!" And he rose and followed Him. (Matt. 9:9)

He also impacted Zaccheus, another tax collector.

And there was a man called by the name of Zaccheus; he was a chief tax collector and he was rich. (Luke 19:2)

> We have staked the whole future of American civilization not upon the power of government, far from it. We have staked the future of all of our political institutions upon the capacity of each and all of us to govern ourselves according to the Ten Commandments of God. —James Madison

Jesus obeyed the laws of the government.

"Is it lawful for us to pay taxes to Caesar, or not?" But He detected their trickery and said to them, "Show Me a denarius. Whose likeness and inscription does it have?" They said, "Caesar's." And He said to them, "Then render to Caesar the things that are Caesar's, and to God the things that are God's." (Luke 20:22–25)

Then the whole body of them got up and brought Him before Pilate. And they began to accuse Him, saying, "We found this man misleading our nation and forbidding to pay taxes to Caesar, and saying that He Himself is Christ, a King." So Pilate asked Him, saying, "Are You the King of the Jews?" And He answered him and said, "It is as you say." Then Pilate said to the chief priests and the crowds, "I find no guilt in this man." (Luke 23:1–4)

A CONSCIENCE FUND

Did you know that ever since 1811 (when someone who had defrauded the government anonymously sent $5 to Washington D.C.) the U.S. Treasury has operated a Conscience Fund? Since that time almost $3.5 million has been received from guilt-ridden citizens.[2]

Even Pilate verified this when the chief priests lied about Jesus to him.

What Are the Enemies of the Habit of Honoring the Government?

1. Distrust—I don't trust the government.
2. Disagreement—I don't agree with the government.
3. Blame—I'm in this mess because of the government.
4. Ignorance—The government is after me.

Make Honoring the Government a Habit

1. Thank God for the government.

Its laws allow you to live in a civil society. Rather than complain about the government, begin thanking God for your country. Thank him for the laws that help to create order within society and offer protection for every citizen.

2. Pray specifically for government leaders—national, state, county, local.

It is our duty to pray for our elected officials. Each day they are confronted with decisions that will affect our lives. Intercession for them is vital if we expect them to make right decisions.

3. Support the military.

Pray for the military. Pray for a strong defense. Do everything possible to express your appreciation for our men and women in uniform. They depend upon our prayers. Military might, as comforting as that is, is no substitute for the power of God that comes as a result of prayer.

4. Pay your taxes.

That is not to suggest that you agree with how your tax money is being spent. It is to suggest that it is our responsibility as citizens, and especially as Christians, to pay our taxes. It allows us to receive the many benefits of living in this great country.

5. Vote your convictions.

Walt Whitman said, "Bad officials are elected by good citizens who do not vote." Christian convictions, not party loyalty, should be the filter through which we cast our votes.

6. Get involved in government.

Run for office or support godly and wise people who do. Ask God how he wants you to get involved. Don't shut out the possibility that he may want you to run for some office or help some candidate get elected.

7. Write to government leaders not only when you disagree or want them to do something, but also to say, "thank you" for what they are doing right.

WEBSTER DIDN'T JUST WRITE A DICTIONARY

One of America's well-known Colonial Americans began his career as a schoolteacher, using the Bible as his most valued textbook. Noah Webster was born in Connecticut and came of age during the American Revolution. He was educated at Yale University, and when he lacked the funds for further studies, he became a teacher. His early impressions of Colonial classrooms were disparaging; they were crowded, disorganized, and poorly equipped. But he continued to teach because he believed the children of our new nation should be taught to honor God's Word and to learn the moral laws in the Scriptures. He also believed that Americans should have American books from which to learn spelling and grammar. His "blue-backed speller" (so nicknamed for its colorful cover) became the standard for schoolchildren for more than one hundred years. He later developed our country's first dictionary because he believed that all Americans should speak distinctly American English not British English. Though Noah Webster is best known for his groundbreaking work with our language, The Presidential Prayer Team acknowledges him for his passion to teach godly values to the schoolchildren of our country. He said, "In my view, the Christian religion is the most important and one of the first things in which all children, under a free government ought to be instructed. . . . No truth is more evident to my mind than that the Christian religion must be the basis of any government intended to secure the rights and privileges of a free people."[3]

There is power in writing a letter. When you disagree with a decision an elected official has made, write to that person and lovingly and tactfully express your opinion. On the other hand, when an elected official makes the right decision, use a letter as an occasion for affirmation.

RED SKELTON THE PROPHET

When Red Skelton was a schoolboy, one of his teachers explained the words and meaning of the pledge of allegiance to his class. Skelton later wrote down, and eventually recorded, his recollection of this lecture. It's followed by an observation of his own.

I—Me; an individual; a committee of one.

Pledge—Dedicate all of my worldly goods to give without self-pity.

Allegiance—My love and my devotion.

To the Flag—Our standard; Old Glory; a symbol of freedom; wherever she waves, there is respect because your loyalty has given her a dignity that shouts, "Freedom is everybody's job."

United—We have all come together.

States—Individual communities that have united into forty-eight great states. Forty-eight individual communities with pride and dignity and purpose. All divided with imaginary boundaries yet united to a common purpose, love for country.

And to the Republic—a state in which sovereign power is invested in representatives chosen by the people to govern. Government is the people; and it's from the people to the leaders, not from the leaders to the people.

For which it stands.

One Nation—Blessed by God.

Indivisible—Incapable of being divided.

With liberty—Freedom; the right of power to live one's own life without threats, fear, or some sort of retaliation.

And justice—The principle, or qualities, of dealing fairly with others.

For all—It's as much your country as it is mine.

Red Skelton then says, "Since I was a small boy, two states have been added to our country, and two words have been added to the pledge of allegiance: 'Under God.' Wouldn't it be a pity if someone said that is a prayer, and that would be eliminated from schools, too?"[4]

8. Send your congressman/woman a nice Bible with his/her name imprinted on it.

You will be amazed at the results of this. Lead your church or a group of Christians to do this. It will be a lasting and impressive gift. There is no greater gift than a Bible.

9. Work to change what's wrong with government instead of complaining about it.

Get proactive. Ask, "How can I help? What can I do to make things better?" Complaining is a negative response with no intention of making things better. Find specific ways you can get involved to bring change.

10. Be in the know on issues facing decision makers.

Read about the issues. Understand decisions that are facing elected officials. Knowledge is powerful. In our society ignorance on the issues is no excuse.

PRAYER AND THE CONSTITUTION

"Go back to the drafting of the U.S. Constitution. It was the summer of 1787, and the representatives who broke free from the tyranny of the British Empire were gathered in Philadelphia to hammer out this great document. After weeks of almost no progress, many were ready to walk away from the convention. Benjamin Franklin, who was eighty-one years old, stood and challenged the leaders with these words: "I have lived, sir, a long time, and the longer I live, the more convincing proofs I see of this truth: that God governs in the affairs of men. And if a sparrow cannot fall to the ground without his notice [which, I should point out, is a direct reference to the words of Jesus in Matthew 10], is it probable that an empire can rise without his aid? We have been assured, sir, in the Sacred Writings, that 'except the Lord build the House, they labor in vain that build it.' I firmly believe this. . . . I, therefore, beg leave to move that, henceforth, prayers imploring the assistance of heaven, and its blessings on our deliberations, be held in this assembly every morning." What's this? The Founding Fathers were challenged to pray every day at the start of government business? How did they respond? They started to pray at their meetings, a tradition the House and the Senate still embrace today."[5]

THE HABIT OF
ASKING QUESTIONS

POINT PASSAGE

*Then, after three days they found Him in the temple,
sitting in the midst of the teachers, both listening to them
and asking them questions.*

LUKE 2:46

The Jesus habit of asking questions is choosing to ask certain things—normally open-ended questions—in order to gain knowledge and understanding.

> Don't be afraid to ask dumb questions. They are easier to handle than dumb mistakes.
>
> —Thomas Fuller

Jesus Showed Us How to Ask Questions

Jesus continually used questions. One of the first pictures of the young Jesus is of him sitting in the temple asking questions. He used questions in a variety of ways for a variety of reasons. These snapshots show us how he used questions.

Jesus used questions to get people to investigate their own lives, to look within, and to discover their need for God.

As they were leaving Jericho, a large crowd followed Him. And two blind men sitting by the road, hearing that Jesus was passing by, cried out, "Lord, have mercy on us, Son of David!" The crowd sternly told them to be quiet, but they cried out all the more, "Lord, Son of David, have mercy on us!" And Jesus stopped and called them, and said, "What do you want Me to do for you?" They said to Him, "Lord, we want our eyes to be opened." Moved with compassion, Jesus touched their eyes; and immediately they regained their sight and followed Him. (Matt. 20:29–34)

Jesus asked the blind man in Jericho, "What do you want me to do for you?" This gave the man the opportunity to see his physical, as well as his spiritual, need and express that need specifically.

Jesus often answered a question with a question.

When He entered the temple, the chief priests and the elders of the people came to Him while He was teaching, and said, "By what authority are You doing these things, and who gave You this authority?" Jesus said to them, "I will also ask you one thing, which if you tell Me, I will also tell you by what authority I do these things. The baptism of John was from what source, from heaven or from men?" And they began reasoning among themselves, saying, "If we say, 'From heaven,' He will say to us, 'Then why did you not believe him?' But if we say, 'From men,' we fear the people; for they all regard John as a prophet." And answering Jesus, they said, "We do not know." He also said to them, "Neither will I tell you by what authority I do these things." (Matt. 21:23–27)

He did it with the chief priests who questioned his authority. Sometimes the best response to a loaded question is another question.

NOT A SIN TO ASK WHY

Jesus cried out on the cross, "My God, my God, why have you forsaken me?" It was a human cry, a cry of desperation, springing from his heart's agony at the prospect of being put into the hands of wicked men and actually becoming sin for you and me. We can never suffer anything like that, yet we do at times feel forsaken and cry, "Why, Lord?"

The psalmist asked why. Job, a blameless man, suffering horrible torments on an ash heap, asked why. It does not seem to me to be sinful to ask the question. What is sinful is resentment against God and his dealings with us.[1]

Jesus used questions to disarm his critics.

"But regarding the resurrection of the dead, have you not read what was spoken to you by God: 'I am the God of Abraham, and the God of Isaac, and the God of Jacob'? He is not the God of the dead but of the living." (Matt. 22:31–32)

He often silenced critics with a question. One question asked in response to a person's criticism could stop the conversation.

Jesus asked people questions about Scripture.

And He began to speak to them in parables: "A man planted a vineyard and put a wall around it, and dug a vat under the wine press and built a tower, and rented it out to vine-growers and went on a journey. At the harvest time he sent a slave to the vine-growers, in order to receive some of the produce of the vineyard from the vine-growers. They took him, and beat him and sent him away empty-handed. Again he sent them another slave, and they wounded him in the head, and treated him shamefully. And he sent another, and that one they killed; and so with many others, beating some and killing others. He had one more to send, a beloved son; he sent him last of all to them, saying, 'They will respect my son.' But those vine-growers said to one another, 'This is the heir; come, let us kill him, and the inheritance will be ours!' They took him, and killed him and threw him out of the vineyard. What will the owner of the vineyard do? He will come and destroy the vine-growers, and will give the vineyard to others. Have you not even read this Scripture: 'The stone which the builders rejected, this became the chief corner stone; this came about from the Lord, and it is marvelous in our eyes'?" (Mark 12:1–11)

You can learn a lot about the Bible by bombarding the passage with questions.

Jesus asked demons a question.

And Jesus asked him, "What is your name?" And he said, "Legion"; for many demons had entered him. (Luke 8:30)

Jesus used questions to discern if something was of the Father or the father of lies.

Jesus asked a question as one of the last things he said while on the cross.

At the ninth hour Jesus cried out with a loud voice, "Eloi, Eloi, lama sabachthani?" which is translated, "My God, My God, why have You forsaken Me?" (Mark 15:34)

Jesus asked God "Why?" It is not a sin to ask God "Why?" as long as you don't question God and his goodness.

> I keep six honest serving men (They taught me all I knew); Their names are What and Why and When and How and Where and Who.
>
> —**Rudyard Kipling**

What Are the Enemies of the Habit of Asking Questions?

1. Pride—I know all I need to know.
2. Fear—I may appear to be stupid. I don't want to know.
3. Lack of concern—I don't care enough to ask.

Make Asking Questions a Habit

1. Ask questions to learn about specific issues in order to grow personally.

Open-ended questions get the greatest response. The reason is, more information is shared. The right question, asked in the right way, can yield great light on any subject.

2. Use questions to express your interest in someone.

A well-placed question can show your genuine concern about someone.

3. When studying the Bible, ask questions to determine its meaning then and how it applies to your life now.

Bombard the passage of Scripture with questions. One question that makes a difference is one that pertains to context. What comes immediately before and immediately after the passage? The most important question is to ask how a Scripture passage relates to life application.

4. Ask the Holy Spirit to determine, "Is it God, Satan, or just me?"

SILLY QUESTIONS

The excerpts which follow appeared in the *Salt Lake Tribune*. They were taken from real court records:

Q: What happened then? A: He told me, he says, "I have to kill you because you can identify me."

Q: Did he kill you?

Q: The youngest son, the 20-year-old, how old is he?

Q: She had three children, right? A: Yes.

Q: How many were boys? A: None. *Q: Were there any girls?*

Q: Were you alone or by yourself?

Q: I show you Exhibit 3 and ask you if you recognize that picture? A: That's me.

Q: Were you present when that picture was taken?

Q: You say that the stairs went down to the basement? A: Yes.

Q: And these stairs, did they go up also?

Q: Do you have any children or anything of that kind?

Q: Mrs. Jones, do you believe you are emotionally stable? A: I used to be.

Q: How many times have you committed suicide?

Q: So, you were gone until you returned?

Q: You don't know what it was, and you didn't know what it looked like, but can you describe it?

Q: Have you lived in this town all your life? A: Not yet.

Actual questions asked of witnesses from the *Massachusetts Bar Association Lawyers Journal*:

Q: Now doctor, isn't it true that when a person dies in his sleep he doesn't know about it until the next morning?

Q: You were there until the time you left, is that true?

Q: Can you describe the individual? A: He was about medium height and had a beard.

Q: Was this a male or a female?

Q: Doctor, how many autopsies have you performed on dead people? A: All my autopsies are performed on dead people.[2]

It is often hard to discern whether something is of God. By asking the Holy Spirit to help you, you are giving him the freedom to guide you to the truth. The Holy Spirit is always faithful to help us clearly hear the true voice of God.

> No man really becomes a fool until he stops asking questions.
> —Charles P. Stenmetz

5. *Use questions to encourage someone.*

Your questions can be a source of encouragement. For example, ask, "How do you accomplish all you do?" or "How do you stay looking so great?" or "What is your secret of success?" These are encouraging questions.

6. *Get people to open up by asking them questions.*

Closed-ended questions will get short, yes-or-no answers and do not encourage further discussion. If you really want to hear someone's heart, ask questions that allow him to share what is on his mind. These kinds of questions invite sharing.

7. *Express frustrations through questions.*

You can express your frustrations by asking questions like, "Can you help me understand this? Why do I feel so frustrated about this? I am having a difficult time with this; can you give me some insight?"

8. *Seek people's advice through questions.*

Questions invite people's advice. In fact, your question grants them permission to give you their opinion about a matter. Make sure, however, that the advice is consistent with Scripture.

9. *Use questions to counsel people.*

You could simply ask someone, "Are you doing alright? Is there something I can do to help you? May I offer my opinion about this?" Even the question, "What do you think about this?" can be a way to set people on the right track.

10. *Use questions to let someone know you have a need.*

We must put our pride aside and simply ask for help. James let us know that we often do without because we do not ask. There is great power in simply asking when it is done with the right motive.

THE HABIT OF
HAVING FUN

POINT PASSAGE

As Jesus went on from there, He saw a man called Matthew, sitting in the tax collector's booth; and He said to him, "Follow Me!" And he got up and followed Him. Then it happened that as Jesus was reclining at the table in the house, behold, many tax collectors and sinners came and were dining with Jesus and His disciples.

MATTHEW 9:9–10

The Jesus habit of having fun is choosing to enjoy the journey to heaven, giving yourselves permission not to take life so seriously all of the time and making laughter part of your daily routine.

> Seek the kind of fun that doesn't make you ashamed the next day.
> —Unknown

The Laughing Jesus, a drawing by Ray Kovac—have you seen it? If not, you simply must. Most of us can recall pictures of Jesus, and most of them portrayed a solemn, sad, sorrowful Jesus. He is hardly ever smiling. That always bothered me because it seemed inconsistent with many of the scenes in the Gospels. That's why *The Laughing Jesus* has become one of my favorite pictures. The artist depicts Jesus laughing enthusiastically. Make no mistake about it, Jesus had fun. He laughed. He didn't just endure life; he enjoyed it. Now that may ruin some people's image of Jesus, and others may even think it borders on blasphemy to suggest that the Son of God had fun. Jesus made others laugh. Jesus was never a killjoy. He didn't seek out those having fun and then say, "Quit it!"

Jesus Showed Us How to Have Fun

Christians should have fun. Now fun shouldn't always be the goal, nor is the Christian life always fun, but fun should be a natural part of the process of walking daily with God. We should be the most fun-loving, fun-experiencing people on the face of the earth. We have everything to celebrate. Some Christians I meet seem to have the misguided idea that we shouldn't have any fun. They seldom if ever smile, and they look with suspicion upon anyone having a good time.

Put *Jesus* and *fun* on the search engine of your computer and you might get something designed for children such as a Jesus gadget like the Jesus Doll. We simply don't think about the two words going together, but they are not oxymorons. Listen to the description Bruce Marchiana provides from "The Footsteps of Jesus."

> Yes, Jesus smiled; yes, Jesus laughed. Jesus smiled wider and laughed heartier than any human being who has ever walked the planet. He was young. He radiated good cheer. Jesus was a man of such merriment, such gladness of heart, such freedom and openness, that He proved irresistible. He became known throughout Galilee for His genuine strength, the sparkle in His eyes, the spring in His gait, the heartiness in His laugh, the genuineness of His touch; His passion, playfulness,

---

BE LIKE A CHILD

When Dan Jansen brought home a gold medal from the Winter Olympics in 1994, he did so with the help of a sports psychologist named James Loehr. In addition to the routine regimen of proper training, healthy eating, and adequate rest, Jansen was also instructed to lighten up and laugh more. Dr. Loehr noted studies that prove humor relaxes the body and relieves stress. He said a lot can be learned from children in that research shows children laugh an unbelievable four hundred times a day on average. This is compared to adults who average fifteen laughs a day.[1]

excitement, and vitality: His JOY! He made a dazzling display of love. He set hearts afire. He was an elated triumphant young man with an incredible quality of life . . . so different from the solemn religious types He constantly encountered.[2]

Jesus Genuinely Enjoyed Life and It Showed
Jesus regularly attended dinner parties.

He went to Matthew's house.

As Jesus went on from there, He saw a man called Matthew, sitting in the tax collector's booth; and He said to him, "Follow Me!" And he got up and followed Him. Then it happened that as Jesus was reclining at the table in the house, behold, many tax collectors and sinners came and were dining with Jesus and His disciples. (Matt. 9:9–10)

He dined in the home of Zaccheus.

When Jesus came to the place, He looked up and said to him, "Zaccheus, hurry and come down, for today I must stay at your house." And he hurried and came down and received Him gladly. When they saw it, they all began to grumble, saying, "He has gone to be the guest of a man who is a sinner." (Luke 19:5–7)

Jesus loved being around people.

> Whence comes this idea that if what we are doing is fun, it can't be God's will? The God who made giraffes, a baby's fingernails, a puppy's tail, a crookneck squash, the bobwhite's call, and a young girl's giggle has a sense of humor. Make no mistake about that.
> —Catherine Marshall

Jesus attended a wedding.

On the third day there was a wedding in Cana of Galilee, and the mother of Jesus was there; and both Jesus and His disciples were invited to the wedding. When the wine ran out, the mother of Jesus said to

Him, "They have no wine." And Jesus said to her, "Woman, what does that have to do with us? My hour has not yet come." His mother said to the servants, "Whatever He says to you, do it." Now there were six stone waterpots set there for the Jewish custom of purification, containing twenty or thirty gallons each. Jesus said to them, "Fill the waterpots with water." So they filled them up to the brim. And He said to them, "Draw some out now and take it to the headwaiter." So they took it to him. When the headwaiter tasted the water which had become wine, and did not know where it came from (but the servants who had drawn the water knew), the headwaiter called the bridegroom, and said to him, "Every man serves the good wine first, and when the people have drunk freely, then he serves the poorer wine; but you have kept the good wine until now." This beginning of His signs Jesus did in Cana of Galilee, and manifested His glory, and His disciples believed in Him. (John 2:1–11)

A Jewish wedding was a happy, cheerful occasion. Jesus felt right at home. He was there along with his mother Mary. In fact, it was in this happy setting Jesus performed his first miracle. Christians should be at home in happy settings.

DAILY DOSE OF LAUGHTER

If laughter could be ordered at the corner drugstore, any doctor would prescribe many laughs every day. A dose of laughter is a combination of stimuli like that of vitamin tablets plus the relaxation of bromides. Laughter is exercise for the diaphragm, which is neg-lected in most exercises except deep breathing. If you could x-ray yourself when you laugh, you would see astonishing results. Your diaphragm goes down, and your lungs expand. You are taking in more oxygen than usual. A surge of power runs from head to toes.[3]

Jesus loved being around children.

And they were bringing even their babies to Him so that He would touch them, but when the disciples saw it, they began rebuking them. But Jesus called for them, saying, "Permit the children to come to Me, and do not hinder them, for the kingdom of God belongs to such as these." (Luke 18:15–16)

Children are happy; they are fun to be around. They know how to laugh and have a good time.

> Laughter can relieve tension, soothe the pain of disappointment, and strengthen the spirit for the formidable tasks that always lie ahead.
> —Dwight D. Eisenhower

Jesus often used humor in his teachings.

To make a point, Jesus sometimes injected humor. Here are two examples:

"And why worry about a speck in the eye of a brother when you have a board in your own? Should you say, 'Friend, let me help you get that speck out of your eye,' when you can't even see because of the board in your own. Hypocrite! First get rid of the board. Then you can see to help your brother." (Matt. 7:3–5 TLB)

"If your child asks for bread, do you trick him with sawdust? If he asks for fish, do you scare him with a live snake on his plate?" (Matt. 7:9–10 MSG)

What Are the Enemies of the Habit of Having Fun?

1. Busyness—I don't have time for fun.
2. Guilt—I will feel guilty if I stop to have fun.
3. Misperception—Christians shouldn't have fun.
4. Ignorance—I don't know how to have fun.

Make "Fun" a Habit

1. Give yourself permission to have some fun. It is God's will for you to have some fun.

Don't feel guilty about it. It is not an oxymoron to say, "Fun Christian." The lack of fun within a Christian's life has often been used as an objection to Christianity. That's why some label it as boring.

2. Realize that the greatest fun occurs within the boundaries of God's will.

Within the will of God is the freedom to enjoy life. The happiest people on earth are Christians walking in the will of God.

> The human race has one really effective weapon, and that is laughter.
> —Mark Twain

3. Learn to laugh at yourself.

Develop a sense of humor. Lighten up! Life without laughter can get boring and monotonous. Don't take yourself so seriously all the time. Do yourself a favor and learn to see the lighter side of life.

4. Keep a clean conscience.

A clear conscience gives you the freedom to enjoy life. A clean mind forms the basis for a fun life. Joy replaces guilt when the conscience is clean.

5. Expose yourself to good, clean comedy.

Watch the old comedy shows such as *The Andy Griffith Show, I Love Lucy,* and the Marx Brothers. Get a book of clean jokes. Read the funny pages.

6. Make sure you have people in your life that know how to have good clean fun.

You need those who can make you laugh. You do yourself a great favor when you spend time with that kind of people. They lift you up rather than drag you down.

7. Find something away from your work that you enjoy doing.

It is vital that you have built in fun moments in your life. You need something to look forward to. There must be a work disconnect or you will burn out. Discovering what gives you a break from your work is different for each person. You will need to experiment to find what does it for you.

8. Use humor to defuse tense situations.

Humor can be an effective tool for cooling hotheads. It can take a tense conversation and bring back a sense of calm. It gives a momentary time-out to regroup our thoughts and come back to an atmosphere of peace.

9. Use fun to make a point. Inserting humor into a conversation can often be used to make a point about an issue.

A point wrapped in humor—even if it is controversial—is often easier to accept.

10. Be on a mission to show the world that being a Christian is fun, in fact, the most fun in life comes from knowing God and walking in his will.

The world often characterizes Christians as those who have no fun. Make it your passion to destroy that caricature and demonstrate to the world that being a Christian is the most happy and fun adventure known to the human spirit.

THE HABIT OF
TRUTH

POINT PASSAGE

"And you will know the truth, and the truth will make you free."
JOHN 8:32

The Jesus habit of truth is choosing consistently to say what is right, do what is right, and live within the will of God.

> Truth is not always popular, but it is always right.
> —Unknown

Jesus Showed Us Truth

Jesus always told the truth, no exceptions. He embodied truth.

"And the Word became flesh, and dwelt among us, and we saw His glory, glory as of the only begotten from the Father, full of grace and truth." (John 1:14)

Jesus said to him, "I am the way, and the truth, and the life; no one comes to the Father but through Me." (John 14:6)

He not only told the truth, but the way he shared it was packaged with love and grace. At times he turned up the firmness meter when sharing the truth.

The Pharisees and Sadducees came up, and testing Jesus, they asked Him to show them a sign from heaven. But He replied to them, "When it is evening, you say, 'It will be fair weather, for the sky is red.' And in the morning, 'There will be a storm today, for the sky is red and threatening.' Do you know how to discern the appearance of the sky, but cannot discern the signs of the times? An evil and adulterous generation seeks after a sign; and a sign will not be given it, except the sign of Jonah." And He left them and went away.

And the disciples came to the other side of the sea, but they had forgotten to bring any bread. And Jesus said to them, "Watch out and beware of the leaven of the Pharisees and Sadducees." They began to discuss this among themselves, saying, "He said that because we did not bring any bread." But Jesus, aware of this, said, "You men of little faith, why do you discuss among yourselves that you have no bread? Do you not yet understand or remember the five loaves of the five thousand, and how many baskets full you picked up? Or the seven loaves of the four thousand, and how many large baskets full you picked up? How is it that you do not understand that I did not speak to you concerning bread? But beware of the leaven of the Pharisees and Sadducees." Then they understood that He did not say to beware of the leaven of bread, but of the teaching of the Pharisees and Sadducees.

Now when Jesus came into the district of Caesarea Philippi, He was asking His disciples, "Who do people say that the Son of Man is?" And they said, "Some say John the Baptist; and others, Elijah; but still others, Jeremiah, or one of the prophets." He said to them, "But who do you

BAGHDAD BOB

As Operation Iraqi Freedom raged, Mohammed al-Sahhaf, Iraq's Minister of Information, daily refuted clear evidence that Iraq was losing the war. On April 6, after coalition forces seized Baghdad's Saddam Airport, renamed it Baghdad International Airport, started flying planes in, and ventured into Baghdad itself, the *Miami Herald* quoted al-Sahhaf saying, "We butchered the force present at the airport." On April 7, after US troops penetrated central Baghdad and stormed Saddam's Republican Palace, the *Washington Post* quoted al-Sahhaf saying, "There is no presence of the American columns in the city of Baghdad at all. . . . We besieged them, and we killed most of them."[1]

say that I am?" Simon Peter answered, "You are the Christ, the Son of the living God." And Jesus said to him, "Blessed are you, Simon Barjona, because flesh and blood did not reveal this to you, but My Father who is in heaven. I also say to you that you are Peter, and upon this rock I will build My church; and the gates of Hades will not over-power it. I will give you the keys of the kingdom of heaven; and whatever you bind on earth shall have been bound in heaven, and whatever you loose on earth shall have been loosed in heaven." Then He warned the disci-ples that they should tell no one that He was the Christ.

From that time Jesus began to show His disciples that He must go to Jerusalem, and suffer many things from the elders and chief priests and scribes, and be killed, and be raised up on the third day. Peter took Him aside and began to rebuke Him, saying, "God forbid it, Lord! This shall never happen to You." But He turned and said to Peter, "Get behind Me, Satan! You are a stumbling block to Me; for you are not setting your mind on God's interests, but man's." (Matt. 16:1–23)

Jesus answered, "You would have no authority over Me, unless it had been given you from above; for this reason he who delivered Me to you has the greater sin." (John 19:11)

Jesus showed us that truth is the boundary for freedom.

"And you will know the truth, and the truth will make you free." (John 8:32)

Jesus modeled the perfect life. He never veered from the truth. He taught and demonstrated that freedom always lies within the boundary of truth. Those who received his truth found a wonderful freedom.

Jesus showed us the source of lies is Satan.

"You are of your father the devil, and you want to do the desires of your father. He was a murderer from the beginning, and does not stand in the truth because there is no truth in him. Whenever he speaks a lie, he speaks from his own nature, for he is a liar and the father of lies." (John 8:44)

Jesus warned that all lies can be traced back to a common source—Satan. Jesus knew that firsthand. He had been the recipient of Satan's lies, but he also was coming to deal with Satan's first lie to Adam and Eve and the eternal damage that did. We are never more like Christ than when we speak and live the truth, but we are never more like Satan than when we lie.

> Our society finds truth too strong a medicine to digest undiluted. In its purest form, truth is not a polite tap on the shoulder; it is a howling reproach. What Moses brought down from Mt. Sinai were not suggestions but Ten Commandments.
> —Ted Koppel

Jesus showed us the importance of sharing the truth at the right times.

Jesus waited until the atmosphere was right to share certain truths. On the Mount of Transfiguration, Jesus revealed who he was to Peter, James, and John.

> Six days later Jesus took with Him Peter and James and John his brother, and led them up on a high mountain by themselves. And He was transfigured before them; and His face shone like the sun, and His garments became as white as light. And behold, Moses and Elijah appeared to them, talking with Him. Peter said to Jesus, "Lord, it is good for us to be here; if You wish, I will make three tabernacles here, one for You, and one for Moses, and one for Elijah." While he was still speaking, a bright cloud overshadowed them, and behold, a voice out of the cloud said, "This is My beloved Son, with whom I am well-pleased; listen to Him!" When the disciples heard this, they fell face down to the ground and were terrified. And Jesus came to them and touched them and said, "Get up, and do not be afraid." And

lifting up their eyes, they saw no one except Jesus Himself alone.

As they were coming down from the mountain, Jesus commanded them, saying, "Tell the vision to no one until the Son of Man has risen from the dead." And His disciples asked Him, "Why then do the scribes say that Elijah must come first?" And He answered and said, "Elijah is coming and will restore all things; but I say to you that Elijah already came, and they did not recognize him, but did to him whatever they wished. So also the Son of Man is going to suffer at their hands." Then the disciples understood that He had spoken to them about John the Baptist. (Matt. 17:1–13)

Jesus affirmed Peter's confession that he was the Son of God.

And Jesus said to him, "Blessed are you, Simon Barjona, because flesh and blood did not reveal this to you, but My Father who is in heaven." (Matt. 16:17)

At the last supper Jesus revealed his coming death and the fact that one of his disciples had betrayed him.

While they were eating, Jesus took some bread, and after a blessing, He broke it and gave it to the disciples, and said, "Take, eat; this is My body." And when He had taken a cup and given thanks, He gave it to them, saying, "Drink from it, all of you; for this is My blood of the covenant, which is poured out for many for forgiveness

DILUTED PRESCRIPTIONS, DILUTED TRUTH

Recently a Kansas City pharmacist was charged with diluting cancer treatment drugs, Gemzar and Taxol, in order to make a larger profit. So far there are twenty felony counts against the pharmacist, Robert Courtney. He admitted to diluting the drugs during a period of time from November 2000 to March 2001. This man held life-saving power in his hands and for the sake of personal gain diluted it to the point where it could not help people. We can do the same with God's life-saving truth.[2]

of sins. But I say to you, I will not drink of this fruit of the vine from now on until that day when I drink it new with you in My Father's kingdom." After singing a hymn, they went out to the Mount of Olives. (Matt. 26:26–30)

Jesus held to absolute truth.

The statements Jesus made left no room for doubt about his belief in absolute truth. You either believed it or you didn't.

Jesus said to him, "I am the way, and the truth, and the life; no one comes to the Father but through Me." (John 14:6)

"Jesus answered and said to them, "Destroy this temple, and in three days I will raise it up." (John 2:19)

"I am the door; if anyone enters through Me, he will be saved, and will go in and out and find pasture." (John 10:9)

What Are the Enemies of the Habit of Truth?

1. Flattery—You look great (yet deny it away from the person).
2. Convenience—The truth makes me responsible to do something.
3. Avoidance—I don't want to deal with it.
4. Restriction—It would cause me to miss out.
5. Rumors—This is what I heard.

Make Truth a Habit

1. Make a commitment to live and tell the truth no matter what.

Let that be the defining conviction of your life. Be married to the truth at all times, even if it means going against political correctness. Truth often contradicts it. Not only is it vital to tell the truth but also to live a life consistent with the truth.

2. Confess to God immediately any thoughts of deceit or desire to lie.

Deal with truth decay quickly. Allowing any untruth in our lives can affect our perspective. Once we know we have been untruthful in word or action, we must aggressively deal with it, seeking God's forgiveness and committing the truth back into our lives.

3. Avoid any form of lying.

Lying takes on many forms. It could be exaggeration, flattery, silence when you should speak up, fraud, or hypocrisy—saying one thing and doing another. A lie is a lie no matter what form it takes.

> God forbid that we should traffic in unlived truth.
> —H. A. Ironside

4. You are not obligated to share everything you know.

Some things are best left unsaid, even though they may be true. We need the wisdom of God to know what needs to be shared and what doesn't. Just because you know it, doesn't mean it needs to be communicated.

5. Know that truth releases the power of freedom into your life.

Truth and freedom are vitally connected. Freedom only comes as a result of embracing the truth. However, once it is embraced, Jesus has promised bondage-breaking power.

6. Confront untruths.

Stand up for the truth. If something is being shared that is untrue, it is your responsibility to set the record straight. Not doing that when you can makes you a party to the untruth.

7. Some truth needs to be shared at the right time.

Never use sharing the truth to embarrass someone. Be sensitive and choose the appropriate time to communicate sensitive matters of truth.

8. Use the right tone and body language when conveying the truth.

Your tone and body language will communicate more forcefully than your words. It can either make people open to the truth, or it will make them defensive and not open to the truth.

9. If you have told an untruth in the past, confess it and set the record straight.

It will be difficult, but it is the right thing to do. God can mightily use this to further his influence. A Christian who confesses, "I messed up, please forgive me, I was wrong," can have a tremendous impact. That could have a great witness in the lives of those who are not Christians.

10. Refuse to compromise on the truth.

Little compromises on truth can lead to more compromises, which eventually break down our character and testimony. Compromise in the little things always invites more compromise until the truths we hold dear eventually become endangered.

You're Not Yourself

Research psychologists have found there are at least three situations when we do not act like ourselves. First, the average person puts on airs when he visits the lobby of a fancy hotel. Next, the typical Jane Doe will try to hide her emotions and bamboozle the salesman when she enters the new-car showroom. And finally, as we take our seat in church or synagogue, we try to fake out the Almighty that we've really been good all week.[3]

THE HABIT OF
REST

POINT PASSAGE

*On that day Jesus went out of the house, and was sitting by the sea.
And great multitudes gathered to Him, so that He got into a boat
and sat down, and the whole multitude was standing on the beach.*
MATTHEW 13:1–2

The Jesus habit of rest is choosing to relax the body on a regular basis through sleep at night and periodic times during the day.

> Sometimes the most spiritual thing a person can do is sleep.
> —Charles H. Spurgeon

Jesus Showed Us How to Rest

The title of the book caught my attention—*When I Relax I Feel Guilty.* I felt a little guilty just reading the title. The author, Tim Hansel, says, "More today than ever, we need to learn how to give ourselves permission to relax, to play, to enjoy life, and to enjoy God for who He is."[1] Someone humorously commented that we live in a society that wonders why God rested on the seventh day.

As a habit, Jesus rested. He relaxed and didn't feel guilty about it. He slept when his body needed it. He got tired, weary, worn out, just as we do. Yet rather than continuing to push his body, he pressed pause and rested. Only one time do we see that Jesus felt distressed. It was when he was in the garden of Gethsemane.

> And He took with Him Peter and the two sons of Zebedee, and began to be grieved and distressed. (Matt. 26:37)

The word *distressed* means troubled. He does understand the stress you are facing. In fact, no one has ever had the magnitude of stress. Jesus faced such a time in the garden of Gethsemane.

Jesus was sitting by the sea.

> That day Jesus went out of the house and was sitting by the sea. And large crowds gathered to Him, so He got into a boat and sat down, and the whole crowd was standing on the beach. (Matt. 13:1–2)

Jesus used this time to reflect and rest his body.

Jesus was sitting on the mountain.

> Departing from there, Jesus went along by the Sea of Galilee, and having gone up on the mountain, He was sitting there. (Matt. 15:29)

Jesus loved the mountain setting for times of rest.

FATIGUE DANGERS

In *The Twenty-Four Hour Society*, Martin Moore-Ede says our most notorious industrial accidents in recent years—Exxon *Valdez*, Three Mile Island, Chernobyl, the fatal navigational error of Korean Air Lines 007—all occurred in the middle of the night. When the USS *Vincennes* shot down an Iranian A300 air-bus killing all 290 people aboard, fatigue-stressed operators in the high-tech Combat Information Center on the carrier misinterpreted radar data and repeatedly told their captain the jet was descending as if to attack when in fact the airliner remained on a normal flight path. In the *Challenger* space shuttle disaster, key NASA officials made the ill-fated decision to go ahead with the launch after working twenty hours straight and getting only two to three hours of sleep the night before. Their error in judgment cost the lives of seven astronauts and nearly killed the US space program. We ignore our need for rest and renewal at the peril of others and ourselves.[2]

Jesus was sitting by the well.

> And Jacob's well was there. So Jesus, being wearied
> from His journey, was sitting thus by the well. It was
> about the sixth hour. (John 4:6)

Jesus was resting and no doubt refreshing Himself with a cool drink of water.

It is no disgrace to rest a bit.
—Gene Fowler

Jesus was asleep in a boat during a fierce storm.

> And behold, there arose a great storm on the sea, so
> that the boat was being covered with the waves; but
> Jesus Himself was asleep. (Matt. 8:24)

Confidence in the Father allowed Jesus to sleep in the midst of the storm. Our faith brings us peace no matter what the storm.

What Are the Enemies of the Habit of Rest

1. Busyness—I just don't have time to rest.
2. Guilt—I will feel guilty.
3. Unrealistic expectations—The job won't get done if I take the time to rest.
4. Overscheduling—I can't stop or I will get so behind I will never get caught up.

Make Rest a Habit

1. Go to bed early enough to get the sleep you need.

The average adult needs eight hours of sleep. Sleep deprivation is becoming a national safety concern. Sleep is the body's way of getting refreshed and ready for a new day filled with God opportunities.

2. Listen to your body.

Your body will communicate to you what it needs. Pay attention to it. Refuse to ignore the warning signals it gives.

3. During times of extreme stress, learn how to push, pause, stop, and rest.

Stress is a killer, and if not dealt with effectively, it will take its toll on your body wearing it down little by little. It's not a matter of whether we will have stress; it is a matter of how we will deal with it. Rest provides a great part of the answer.

4. When you go to bed at night, by an act of your will, in faith, turn over every concern to the Lord.

Unload your cares. Be comforted that God will be up all night long. Leave your worries with him while you sleep. He can handle it!

5. Take a nap.

Many of the great leaders throughout the centuries understood the power of simply taking a nap. Just a few minutes can make all the difference in your day.

6. Identify your major points of stress.

Pray over each of them asking God for wisdom. Ask God to help you know the best way specifically to deal with your points of stress. When you are aware of your greatest stressors and the times they are most likely to show up in your life, you can more easily manage it.

SLEEPLESS IN AMERICA

Highlights from the National Sleep Foundation's 2001 Sleep in America telephone survey of 1,004 adults:

- 63 percent of the surveyed adults get less than the recommended eight hours of sleep per night; 31 percent get less than seven hours.
- 40 percent of surveyed adults in the U.S. report having trouble staying awake during the day.
- Over the last five years, people in the U.S. have worked more and slept less.

- Eight out of ten people said that they would sleep more if they knew it would improve their health and memory.
- Sleep disorders affect up to seventy million people in the United States. This costs about $100 billion each year in accidents, medical bills, and lost work. (Statistic from *Brain Facts*, Society for Neuroscience, 2002)
- Sleepwalking is also known as "somnambulism"; sleep talking is also known as "somniloquy."[3]

7. Remove yourself geographically from your job periodically for rest.

Proper rest will give you a different perspective. Things often look better from a distance.

8. Find a hobby, something you enjoy doing, something that brings you mental rest.

> Take rest; a field that has rested gives a bountiful crop.
> —Ovid

It is different for every person. It only has to be something that meets your needs. You may have to experiment, but you can find something that recharges you physically and emotionally.

9. Practice the Sabbath—at least one day a week for rest.

God designed the creation that way. He designed our bodies that way. We need at least one day to allow the body to back off from a busy schedule.

10. Get a good checkup from the doctor to determine if there is a physiological or emotional issue preventing you from resting.

A checkup can detect areas where your body can improve. If you have an emotional issue, consider talking with a Christian psychologist. God wants us to be our best, and to get there it may require that we confront both physical and emotional issues.

SHARP AXE OR DULL AXE?

The story is told of two men who had the tiring job of clearing a field of trees. The contract called for them to be paid per tree. Bill wanted the day to be profitable, so he grunted and sweated, swinging the axe relentlessly. Ed, on the other hand, seemed to be working about half as fast. He even took a rest and sat off to the side for a few minutes. Bill kept chopping away until every muscle and tendon in his body was screaming. At the end of the day, Bill was terribly sore, but Ed was smiling and telling jokes. Amazingly, Ed had cut down more trees! Bill said, "I noticed you sitting while I worked without a break. How'd you outwork me?" Ed smiles. "Did you notice I was sharpening my axe while I was sitting?"[4]

THE HABIT OF
ACTING LIKE A MAN

POINT PASSAGE

For He grew up before Him like a tender shoot,
And like a root out of parched ground;
He has no stately form or majesty
That we should look upon Him,
Nor appearance that we should be attracted to Him.
ISAIAH 53:2

The Jesus habit of acting like a man is choosing as a man to be physically strong, emotionally caring, mentally expanding, and spiritually growing.

Jesus Showed Us about Acting Like a Man

Jesus was the consummate man of steel and velvet. He was a real man, the most real man that has ever lived. He was not a macho man, but he was a man's man. There was nothing about Jesus' appearance that would make people look at him and be physically attracted to him. Isaiah tells us:

For He grew up before Him like a tender shoot,
And like a root out of parched ground;
He has no stately form or majesty
That we should look upon Him,

Someone once asked Dr. Albert Schweitzer, "What's wrong with men today?" After a brief pause he said, "The trouble with men today is that they simply don't think."
—Dr. Albert Schweitzer[1]

148

Nor appearance that we should be attracted to Him.
(Isa. 53:2)

However, people were attracted to him, the person.

Men in our society seem to be confused about manhood. What is a man and what is he supposed to act like? Think about some of the role models we have had—Archie Bunker, Tim the Tool Man Taylor, and his sidekick Al Borland, Homer Simpson, Sylvester Stalone, Ray Barone of *Everybody Loves Raymond*.

Jesus needs to be our role model.

Jesus was strong enough to carry his own cross yet gentle enough to allow children to sit on his lap.

They took Jesus therefore, and He went out, bearing His own cross, to the place called the Place of the Skull. (John 19:17)

Then some children were brought to Him so that He might lay His hands on them and pray; and the disciples rebuked them. (Matt. 19:13)

Jesus was very tender and gentle with children.

THE AVERAGE MALE

The average male is: 5 feet 9 inches tall and 173 pounds. He is married, 1.8 years older than his wife, and would marry her again. He has not completed college. He earns $28,605 per year. He prefers showering to taking a bath. He spends about 7.2 hours a week eating. He does not know his cholesterol count, but it's 211. He watches 26 hours and 44 minutes of TV a week. He takes out the garbage in his household. He prefers white underwear to colored. He cries about once a month, one fourth as much as Jane Doe. He falls in love an average of six times during his life. He eats his corn on the cob in circles, not straight across and prefers his steak medium. He can't whistle by inserting his fingers in his mouth. He prefers that his toilet tissue unwind over rather than under. He has sex 2.55 times a week. He daydreams mostly about sex. He thinks he looks OK in the nude. And he will not stop to ask for directions when he's in the car.[2]

Jesus was strong enough to stand up to the Pharisees and tell them like it was yet gentle enough to allow a woman to pour perfume on him

"But woe to you, scribes and Pharisees, hypocrites, because you shut off the kingdom of heaven from people; for you do not enter in yourselves, nor do you allow those who are entering to go in. Woe to you, scribes and Pharisees, hypocrites, because you devour widows' houses, and for a pretense you make long prayers; therefore you will receive greater condemnation.

"Woe to you, scribes and Pharisees, hypocrites, because you travel around on sea and land to make one proselyte; and when he becomes one, you make him twice as much a son of hell as yourselves.

"Woe to you, blind guides, who say, 'Whoever swears by the temple, that is nothing; but whoever swears by the gold of the temple is obligated.' You fools and blind men! Which is more important, the gold or

HOMES IN NEED OF SPIRITUAL LEADERS

Recent research is shining light on the importance of male spiritual leadership in the home. Among their findings is the reality that sixty-eight million of our nation's ninety-four million men don't attend any church. This, in spite of the fact, that 86 percent of them grew up with some sort of church background. Research has revealed that if a child is the first person in a household to become a Christian, there is only a 3.5 percent probability that everyone else in the household will become Christians. If the mother is the first to accept Christ, the percent goes up; 17 percent of the homes will see the remainder of its members trust Christ. But if the father is first, there is a 93 percent probability that everyone else in the household will follow. When father goes first spiritually, good things happen at home. Let's all pray together that God will call even more men to spiritual revival and renewal. Never has there been a generation in our nation when this has been more important than now.[3]

the temple that sanctified the gold? And, 'Whoever swears by the altar, that is nothing, but whoever swears by the offering on it, he is obligated.' You blind men, which is more important, the offering, or the altar that sanctifies the offering? Therefore, whoever swears by the altar, swears both by the altar and by everything on it. And whoever swears by the temple, swears both by the temple and by Him who dwells within it. And whoever swears by heaven, swears both by the throne of God and by Him who sits upon it.

"Woe to you, scribes and Pharisees, hypocrites! For you tithe mint and dill and cummin, and have neglected the weightier provisions of the law: justice and mercy and faithfulness; but these are the things you should have done without neglecting the others. You blind guides, who strain out a gnat and swallow a camel!

"Woe to you, scribes and Pharisees, hypocrites! For you clean the outside of the cup and of the dish, but inside they are full of robbery and self-indulgence. You blind Pharisee, first clean the inside of the cup and of the dish, so that the outside of it may become clean also.

"Woe to you, scribes and Pharisees, hypocrites! For you are like whitewashed tombs which on the outside appear beautiful, but inside they are full of dead men's bones and all uncleanness. So you, too, outwardly appear righteous to men, but inwardly you are full of hypocrisy and lawlessness. Woe to you, scribes and Pharisees, hypocrites! For you build the tombs of the prophets and adorn the monuments of the righteous, and say, 'If we had been living in the days of our fathers, we would not have been partners with them in shedding the blood of the prophets.' So you testify against yourselves, that you are sons of those who murdered the prophets. Fill up, then, the measure of the guilt of your fathers. You serpents, you brood of vipers, how will you escape the sentence of hell?

"Therefore, behold, I am sending you prophets and wise men and scribes; some of them you will kill and crucify, and some of them you will scourge in your synagogues, and persecute from city to city, so that upon you may fall the guilt of all the righteous blood shed on earth, from the blood of righteous Abel to the blood of Zechariah, the son of Berechiah, whom you murdered between the temple and the altar. Truly I say to you, all these things will come upon this generation." (Matt. 23:13–36)

Now when Jesus was in Bethany, at the home of Simon the leper, a woman came to Him with an alabaster vial of very costly perfume, and she poured it on His head as He reclined at the table. But the disciples were indignant when they saw this, and said, "Why this waste? For this perfume might have been sold for a high price and the money given to the poor." But Jesus, aware of this, said to them, "Why do you bother the woman? For she has done a good deed to Me. For you always have the poor with you; but you do not always have Me. For when she poured this perfume on My body, she did it to prepare Me for burial. Truly I say to you, wherever this gospel is preached in the whole world, what this woman has done will also be spoken of in memory of her." (Matt. 26:6–13)

Jesus was strong enough to run out those money changers who were abusing God's house, yet gentle enough to cry at the death of his friend Lazarus.

And Jesus entered the temple and drove out all those who were buying and selling in the temple, and overturned the tables of the moneychangers and the seats of those who were selling doves. (Matt. 21:12)

Jesus wept. (John 11:35)

Jesus was intelligent enough to deal with the intellectual Nicodemus, yet he was one of the guys enough to go fishing.

Now there was a man of the Pharisees, named Nicodemus, a ruler of the Jews; this man came to Jesus by night and said to Him, "Rabbi, we know that You have come from God as a teacher; for no one can do these signs that You do unless God is with him." Jesus answered and said to him, "Truly, truly, I say to you, unless one is born again he cannot see the kingdom of God."

Nicodemus said to Him, "How can a man be born when he is old? He cannot enter a second time into his mother's womb and be born, can he?" Jesus answered, "Truly, truly, I say to you, unless one is born of water and the Spirit he cannot enter into the kingdom of God. That which is born of the flesh is flesh, and that which is born of the Spirit is spirit. Do not be amazed that

THE WORLD NEEDS MEN

The World Needs Men . . .
- who cannot be bought.
- whose word is their bond.
- who put character above wealth.
- who possess opinions and a will.
- who are larger than their vocations.
- who do not hesitate to take chances.
- who will not lose their individuality in a crowd.
- who will be as honest in small things as in great things.
- who will make no compromise with wrong.
- whose ambitions are not confined in their own selfish desires.
- who will not say they do it "because everybody else is doing it."
- who are true to their friends through both good and evil reports, in adversity as well as in prosperity.
- who do not believe that shrewdness, cunning, and hardheadedness are the best qualities for winning success.
- who are not ashamed or afraid to stand for the truth when it is unpopular.
- who say no with emphasis, although the rest of the world says yes.[4]

I said to you, 'You must be born again.' The wind blows where it wishes and you hear the sound of it, but do not know where it comes from and where it is going; so is everyone who is born of the Spirit."

Nicodemus said to Him, "How can these things be?" Jesus answered and said to him, "Are you the teacher of Israel and do not understand these things? Truly, truly, I say to you, we speak of what we know and testify of what we have seen, and you do not accept our testimony. If I told you earthly things and you do not believe, how will you believe if I tell you heavenly things? No one has ascended into heaven, but He

> Be on the alert, stand firm in the faith, act like men, be strong.
> —1 Cor. 16:13

who descended from heaven: the Son of Man. As Moses lifted up the serpent in the wilderness, even so must the Son of Man be lifted up; so that whoever believes will in Him have eternal life. For God so loved the world, that He gave His only begotten Son, that whoever believes in Him shall not perish, but have eternal life.

"For God did not send the Son into the world to judge the world, but that the world might be saved through Him. He who believes in Him is not judged; he who does not believe has been judged already, because he has not believed in the name of the only begotten Son of God. This is the judgment, that the Light has come into the world, and men loved the darkness rather than the Light, for their deeds were evil. For everyone who does evil hates the Light, and does not come to the Light for fear that his deeds will be exposed. But he who practices the truth comes to the Light, so that his deeds may be manifested as having been wrought in God." (John 3:1–21)

Now it happened that while the crowd was pressing around Him and listening to the word of God, He was standing by the lake of Gennesaret; and He saw two boats lying at the edge of the lake; but the fishermen had gotten out of them and were washing their nets. And He got into one of the boats, which was Simon's, and asked him to put out a little way from the land. And He sat down and began teaching the people from the boat. When He had finished speaking, He said to Simon, "Put out into the deep water and let down your nets for a catch." Simon answered and said, "Master, we worked hard all night and caught nothing, but I will do as You say and let down the nets." When they had done this, they enclosed a great quantity of fish, and their nets began to break; so they signaled to their partners in the other boat for them to come and help them. And they came and filled both of the boats, so that they began to sink. (Luke 5:1–7)

Jesus withstood unbearable beatings and death on the cross. He died like a man yet until his death he remained sensitive to the needs of others.

Then the soldiers of the governor took Jesus into the Praetorium and gathered the whole Roman cohort around Him. They stripped Him and put a scarlet robe on Him. And after twisting together a crown of thorns, they put it on His head, and a reed in His right hand; and they knelt down before Him and mocked Him, saying, "Hail, King of the Jews!" They spat on Him, and took the reed and began to beat Him on the head. After they had mocked Him, they took the scarlet robe off Him and put His own garments back on Him, and led Him away to crucify Him. As they were coming out, they found a man of Cyrene named Simon, whom they pressed into service to bear His cross. (Matt. 27:27–32)

When Jesus then saw His mother, and the disciple whom He loved standing nearby, He said to His mother, "Woman, behold, your son!" Then He said to the disciple, "Behold, your mother!" From that hour the disciple took her into his own household. (John 19:26–27)

Jesus had all power in his possession, yet on the cross he chose to suffer because of his love for sinners.

"Or do you think that I cannot appeal to My Father, and He will at once put at My disposal more than twelve legions of angels?" (Matt. 26:53)

A legion is six thousand. Jesus is saying that he could have called down seventy-two thousand angels. Being a real man is strength under control.

THE REAL DIFFERENCE BETWEEN MEN AND WOMEN

NICKNAMES

If Laura, Suzanne, Debra, and Rose go out for lunch, they will call each other Laura, Suzanne, Debra, and Rose.

If Mike, Charlie, Bob, and John go out, they will affectionately refer to each other as Fat Boy, Godzilla, Peanut-Head, and Scrappy.

EATING OUT

When the bill arrives, Mike, Charlie, Bob, and John will each throw in $20, even though it's only for $32.50. None of them will have anything smaller, and none will actually admit they want change back.

When the girls get their bill, out come the pocket calculators.

MONEY

A man will pay $2.00 for a $2.00 item he wants.

A woman will pay $1.00 for a $2.00 item that she doesn't want.

BATHROOMS

A man has five items in his bathroom: a toothbrush, shaving cream, a razor, a bar of soap, and a towel from the Holiday Inn.

The average number of items in the typical woman's bathroom is 337. A man would not be able to identify most of these items.

MARRIAGE

A woman marries a man expecting he will change, but he doesn't.

A man marries a woman expecting that she won't change and she does.

OFFSPRING

Ah, children. A woman knows all about her children. She knows about dentist appointments and romances, best friends, favorite foods, secret fears, and hopes and dreams. A man is vaguely aware of some short people living in the house.[5]

What Are the Enemies of the Habit of Acting Like a Man?

1. Confusion—How should I act?
2. Roles—What am I supposed to do?
3. Culture—My wife is capable of handling decisions on her own.
4. Abdication—I don't want the responsibility.

Make Acting Like a Man a Habit

1. A real man is loving, kind, gentle, and sensitive.

Gentleness may be the most attractive characteristic a man can possess. It is strength under the control of grace.

2. A real man can cry.

To suggest that real men don't cry is to deny that Jesus was also a man. Tears can express a man's compassion toward someone or burden for someone. A man should not be embarrassed by his tears.

3. A real man is released from the pressure of acting macho, but he does things that reflect his manhood.

Macho is a negative term suggesting that a man has to act a certain way in order to be accepted by other men. A real man acts like a man but is secure enough within himself that he doesn't always have to prove that he is a man.

4. A real man respects women.

He will go out of his way to show the value he sees in women. It is reflected in his speech with women and about women. This attitude is seen in his daily interactions with the women within his sphere of relationships.

5. A real man takes an active role in raising his children.

It is not just the woman's place to raise the children. A man should take a proactive approach in helping to raise children. That involves not just the big events of life but also the day-to-day tasks.

6. A real man grows spiritually.

He will constantly be going forward in his faith. He is concerned about reading the Bible and praying daily, as well as being involved in a church.

7. A real man takes care of his body.

He does everything possible to take care of his body. He sets the example by refusing to put anything in his body that will damage it. He works on his weight through a healthy diet and exercise. He strives to get enough rest.

8. A real man is faithful to his wife.

He takes the wedding vows he made to his wife seriously. A real man will, like Job, make a covenant with his eyes not to look on another woman with lust. He is faithful to carry out his duties as a husband to the woman he married.

9. A real man doesn't intentionally put himself in a place where he could easily give in to temptation.

He avoids situations that encourage letting down one's spiritual and moral guard. He guards his heart against anything that threatens his purity. Further, he immediately deals with impure thoughts.

10. A real man looks nice but is not overly preoccupied with his appearance.

A man should do everything possible to strive for excellence in his appearance, the way he keeps himself. However, he will not allow vanity to control him. In our society this will be a constant but winnable battle.

THE HABIT OF
ESTEEMING
WOMEN

POINT PASSAGE

Straightening up, Jesus said to her, "Woman, where are they?
Did no one condemn you?" She said, "No one, Lord."
And Jesus said, "I do not condemn you, either.
Go. From now on sin no more."
JOHN 8:10–11

The Jesus habit of esteeming women is choosing to treat all women, at all times, with the utmost dignity and respect they deserve.

> One can judge a civilization by the way it treats its women.
> —**Helen Foster Snow**[1]

Jesus Showed Us How to Esteem Women

Jesus elevated womanhood to its highest level. No one could ever accuse Jesus of treating women with anything but respect and dignity. His teachings backed that up as well. To know how to treat women, look to Jesus, the consummate example.

Jesus valued women the same as he did men.

Now Jesus loved Martha and her sister and Lazarus. (John 11:5)

Women played a strategic role in Jesus' life and ministry. Some of his closest friends were women—Martha and Mary. Jesus also valued the wisdom of women. He listened to their opinions and their advice.

Jesus listened to women.

When the wine ran out, the mother of Jesus said to Him, "They have no wine." And Jesus said to her, "Woman, what does that have to do with us? My hour has not yet come." His mother said to the servants, "Whatever He says to you, do it." Now there were six stone waterpots set there for the Jewish custom of purification, containing twenty or thirty gallons each. Jesus said to them, "Fill the waterpots with water." So they filled them up to the brim. (John 2:3–7)

Jesus listened to his mother as she presented a need to him.

Jesus respected women.

Therefore the soldiers did these things. But standing by the cross of Jesus were His mother, and His mother's sister, Mary the wife of Clopas, and Mary Magdalene. (John 19:25)

Jesus respected their commitment to his cause and their courage to stand with him during his darkest hours.

When the Sabbath was over, Mary Magdalene, and Mary the mother of James, and Salome, bought spices, so that they might come and anoint Him. Very early on the first day of the week, they came to the tomb when the sun had risen. They were saying to one another, "Who will roll away the stone for us from the entrance of the tomb?" (Mark 16:1–3)

UNDER THE INFLUENCE

In the book, *Under the Influence, How Christianity Transformed Civilization,* Alvin J. Schmidt, observes: "The birth of Jesus was the turning point in the history of woman. Whatever else our Lord did, he immeasurably exalted womanhood. Yet neither Christ nor the early Christians ever preached an outright revolution. Rather, it was his example that his followers reflected in their relationships with women, raising their dignity, freedom, and right to a level previously unknown in any culture."[2]

When Jesus rose from the dead, the women were there.

Now after He had risen early on the first day of the week, He first appeared to Mary Magdalene, from whom He had cast out seven demons. She went and reported to those who had been with Him, while they were mourning and weeping. (Mark 16:9–10)

It was a woman who went to tell Peter and John that Jesus' body was gone from the tomb.

Jesus affirmed women.

Straightening up, Jesus said to her, "Woman, where are they? Did no one condemn you?" She said, "No one, Lord." And Jesus said, "I do not condemn you, either. Go. From now on sin no more." (John 8:10–11)

Jesus affirmed this woman's worth in spite of her sinfulness. He brought her wholeness and dignity again.

Jesus defended women.

But when they persisted in asking Him, He straightened up, and said to them, "He who is without sin among you, let him be the first to throw a stone at her." (John 8:7)

LOOKING FOR MR. RIGHT

Scholars from the Institute for American Values conducted a survey, "Hooking Up, Hanging Out, and Looking for Mr. Right," that asked one thousand college women about courtship in the new millennium. The survey found that courtship—dating a male with the hopes of finding a lifelong mate—has been replaced by "hooking up." Hooking up with a male partner usually is fueled by alcohol and entails engaging in sexual activity. Forty percent of the women surveyed admitted to hooking up with men, and one in ten disclosed they'd done so at least six times. Elizabeth Marquardt, coauthor of the report says, "The women wish they could really get to know a guy without necessarily having a sexual relationship." This survey was conducted after the National Marriage Project at Rutgers University released a report in 1999 that concluded that Americans are marrying far less, and those who do marry are less happy.[3]

Jesus defended women against men who would abuse them or mistreat them. He would not tolerate abuse verbally, emotionally, or physically against women.

Jesus chose to reveal eternal truths to women.

Jesus said to her, "I am the resurrection and the life; he who believes in Me will live even if he dies, and everyone who lives and believes in Me will never die. Do you believe this?" (John 11:25–26)

To Martha, Jesus revealed his resurrection.

The first evangelist in the Bible was a woman, the woman at the well who received Christ.

So the woman left her waterpot, and went into the city and said to the men, "Come, see a man who told me all the things that I have done; this is not the Christ, is it?" (John 4:28–29)

What Are the Enemies of Esteeming Women?

1. Seeing them as sex objects—I'm not in love, just in lust.
2. Feminism—Women don't need men.
3. Abuse—I can treat her any way I want to.
4. Machismo—A woman's job is to serve men.

PROVERBS 31 WOMEN

Throughout history, women have been treated by men as lesser humans. Athenian women were of inferior status, often guarded by dogs, treated as fickle, contentious, and uncultured in comedy. In Jesus' day there was a prayer said by Jewish men thanking God in this manner, "Thank you for not making me an unbeliever or barbarian, a slave, or a woman." Application: Without the gospel, no man could ever have a proper view of what a true blessing a wife is. In Proverbs 31, the chapter on the virtuous wife, the husband is given this example of recognizing his wife as a gift, "Her children arise and call her blessed; her husband also, and he praises her . . . a woman who fears the LORD is to be praised." Give her the reward she has earned.[4]

Make Esteeming Women a Habit

1. Treat every woman like a lady.

Go out of your way to assist her. Be nice to women. Be kind. Be a gentleman. Respect every woman.

2. Treat every woman as an intellectual equal.

Never treat a woman as if she is inferior. She is certainly not inferior.

3. No woman is your slave.

Women are not properties a man possesses; they are people who should be respected as equals. Often men have understood the principle of "wives obey" to mean, "wives are slaves." No woman is a slave.

4. Appreciate women.

They are multitask oriented; men usually are not. Appreciate women for all they can do and for how quickly and effectively they can do it. Further, appreciate the many things required of them as wife, mother, and worker.

> "Let the wife make the husband glad to come home, and let him make her sorry to see him leave."
> —**Martin Luther**

5. See every woman, except your wife, as a sister or mother.

Women aren't sex objects, although our society has attempted to make them so. Men must daily commit their minds to God so that lust never has an opportunity to gain a stronghold.

6. Put away anything in your life that demeans women.

Pornography is an example. There is no place in the Christian life for anything that in any way lessens God's value of women. That includes suggestive talk or humor concerning women.

7. Stand up against anything that hurts women.

We should never allow anything that is hurting a woman or women to go unchallenged. Men should always be on the watch for how they can assist women and make certain they are treated with the utmost respect.

8. Affirm women who are making a difference.

Thank God for those women who are making an impact on our society for God. Had it not been for women, many churches and faith-based organizations would not exist. Take time to write a note or say thank you to those women.

9. Learn from women.

They have much to teach men. Men shouldn't feel threatened by this at all. In every fiber of our beings, men and women are different. Men can learn great lessons for life by observing women. A smart man learns from them.

10. Begin by treating your wife or your daughter with the utmost love, care, and understanding.

Esteeming women begins by valuing the women who live in your home. Let your home be a place where the women are treated better there than they are treated in any other place.

A TEN-COW WIFE

Johnny Lingo lived many years ago on the island of Oahu, Hawaii. He was known as a trader, a man who could get anything for you at a price lower than anyone else could manage. He was smart and cagey, and he could negotiate better than any man on the island. This ability had made him very rich and equally well respected.

It was the custom at this time for men to offer the fathers of their prospective wives a certain number of cows in exchange for their daughters' hand in marriage. The standard price was three cows, and most deals were struck for that price. Every once in a great while a girl would go for four cows, but she would be exceptionally beautiful and very much in demand. There was even an unsubstantiated rumor that a young girl with truly beautiful features, great charm, and strong character had gone for five cows, but no one could remember her name or the details of the match.

One man on the island lived with his two daughters. The younger one was very pretty and desirable. She was at least a three-cow bride, perhaps four. Her older sister, still unmarried, was not very attractive at all, and her father had little hope of getting even two cows for her. He had decided some time before that if a suitor came who offered one cow, he would let her be taken for that, but no one came to call.

One day Johnny Lingo came to this man's house. Everyone assumed he was calling for the younger girl, and people began to speculate. The girl was ravishing, but no one could bargain like Johnny Lingo. Who would come out on top—Johnny or the girl's father? Would Johnny hold out for a low price of three cows? Would her father insist on no less than four? Everyone on the island was breathless in anticipation of the negotiations.

Then something strange happened. Johnny Lingo asked to see the older daughter! Her father was dumbfounded. He thought perhaps he had misunderstood. Surely Johnny meant his younger daughter? "No," Johnny said. "The older." He would not be swayed. The old man was beside himself with joy! His worst fear was that he would be forced to give the girl away, but now the richest man on the island was inquiring about her. Everyone knew that Johnny was as generous as he was rich, and they began to speculate about the price he would give for this homely daughter. Surely he would pay at least the standard three-cow price!

Then again, maybe just to make a point, he would offer four cows. Or perhaps, just to say that no one had paid more for a wife than Johnny Lingo, he would offer five cows!

Can you imagine the shock when hard-bargaining John Lingo offered ten cows for the least desirable girl on the island? Her father was beside himself. He quickly agreed and hastily arranged the marriage, fearing that Johnny would realize the extravagance of his offer and back out of the deal. Johnny had no such intent. He just smiled, paid the ten cows, and announced that

he and his ten-cow wife were going on a two-year honeymoon and would return after that to make their home on the island.

Two years passed, and then a lookout was posted to search the horizon for the returning bride and groom. He spotted Johnny easily. Everyone knew Johnny, but he wasn't sure that this was the same woman he had left the island with. She was vaguely familiar but so incredibly beautiful that it was hard to believe she was the one. She walked with confidence; she was gracious and self-assured. And when the town gathered around them, all who were there agreed that the change in Johnny's bride was unbelievable. Those who had laughed for months over the price he paid were now saying what a bargain he had gotten! Many agreed they would have paid twenty cows for a woman this attractive.

What happened? What changed this woman from an unattractive wallflower to a compelling, vital, beautiful, ten-cow bride? The same thing that happens today when a man treats his wife as the woman he desires her to be. Goethe said, "If you treat a man as he is, he will stay as he is. If you treat him as if he were bigger than he ought to be, he will become that bigger and better man." The same is true of any woman alive. Husbands, do you want an attractive wife? Let her know that she is beautiful in your eyes and watch her blossom into the beauty that God created her to be![5]

THE HABIT OF
GIVING

POINT PASSAGE

"For God so loved the world,
that He gave His only begotten Son, that whoever
believes in Him shall not perish, but have eternal life."
JOHN 3:16

The Jesus habit of giving is choosing as a way of life to offer yourself, your time, money, and resources on behalf of others in the name of Jesus.

> When we come to the end of life, the question will be, How much have you given? not, How much have you gotten?
> —**George Sweeting**

Jesus Showed Us How to Give

Jesus was a giver, not a taker. It was all about others. Every time you see Jesus you see Him giving to others. There was not one ounce of selfishness in Him. The ultimate act of giving was when He gave Himself on the cross for the sin of the world.

Jesus gave life.

Now as He approached the gate of the city, a dead man was being carried out, the only son of his mother, and she was a widow; and a sizeable crowd from the city was with her. When the Lord saw her, He felt compassion for her, and said to her, "Do not weep." And He came up and touched the coffin; and the bearers came to a halt. And He said, "Young man, I say to you, arise!"

The dead man sat up and began to speak. And Jesus gave him back to his mother. (Luke 7:12–15)

Jesus touched the coffin of a dead son and gave him life.

Jesus gave sight to the blind.

At that very time He cured many people of diseases and afflictions and evil spirits; and He gave sight to many who were blind. (Luke 7:21)

Jesus gave power.

And He called the twelve together, and gave them power and authority over all the demons and to heal diseases. (Luke 9:1)

OTHERS!

I read biographies a great deal. Especially in the early, formative days of my ministry, I often read biographies. I have read about the lives of most great men. One of my favorite characters in all of history is General William Booth. General Booth was the founder of the great Salvation Army. He led in spreading the gospel over much of the world, as he organized street meetings and evangelistic services.

With the passing of the years, General Booth became an invalid. His eyesight failed him, and one year he was in such bad health that he was unable to attend the Salvation Army Convention in London, England. Somebody suggested that General Booth send a telegram or a message to be read at the opening of the convention. General Booth agreed to do so.

When the thousands of delegates met, the moderator announced that General Booth would not be able to be present because of failing health and eyesight. Gloom and pessimism swept across the floor of the convention. A little light dispelled some of the darkness when the moderator announced that General Booth had sent a message to be read with the opening of the first session. He opened the message and began to read the following:

Dear Delegates of the Salvation Army Convention:
OTHERS!
Signed, General Booth[1]

Jesus gave food.

When He had reclined at the table with them, He took the bread and blessed it, and breaking it, He began giving it to them. (Luke 24:30)

Jesus gave to his enemies.

Jesus then answered, "That is the one for whom I shall dip the morsel and give it to him." So when He had dipped the morsel, He took and gave it to Judas, the son of Simon Iscariot. (John 13:26)

> **The Dead Sea is the dead sea because it continually receives and never gives.**
> **—Unknown**

Jesus gave his love.

"This is My commandment, that you love one another, just as I have loved you. Greater love has no one than this, that one lay down his life for his friends." (John 15:12–13)

Jesus gave light.

Then Jesus again spoke to them, saying, "I am the Light of the world; he who follows Me will not walk in the darkness, but will have the Light of life." (John 8:12)

So Jesus said to them, "For a little while longer the Light is among you. Walk while you have the Light, so that darkness will not overtake you; he who walks in the darkness does not know where he goes." (John 12:35)

Jesus gave his life.

"For even the Son of Man did not come to be served, but to serve, and to give His life a ransom for many." (Mark 10:45)

And Jesus, crying out with a loud voice, said, "Father, into Your hands I commit My spirit." Having said this, He breathed His last. (Luke 23:46)

Jesus said to her, "I am the resurrection and the life; he who believes in Me will live even if he dies." (John 11:25)

What Are the Enemies of the Habit of Giving?

Selfishness—What about me?

Greed—What's in it for me?

Attitude—What has anybody ever done for me?

Make Giving a Habit

1. Choose to be a giver and not a taker.

> You are never more like God than when you give.
> —Unknown

Givers are glad, and misers are miserable. Giving begins with an attitude that says, "I will be a giver and not a taker." Every act of giving you see in others comes as a result of a choice to do so.

2. Every day place self-centeredness on the altar.

By nature we all tend to be self-centered, possessing a "what's in it for me" mind-set. It is a constant battle that requires a continual going to the altar and placing self on it. Be reminded that when you place self on the altar, it quickly sprouts legs and feet and crawls off the altar. This is a continual exercise.

THE FLINT, THE SPONGE, AND THE HONEYCOMB

Givers can be divided into three types: the flint, the sponge, and the honeycomb. Some givers are like a piece of flint—to get anything out of it you must hammer it, and even then you get only chips and sparks. Others are like a sponge—to get anything out of a sponge you must squeeze it and squeeze it hard because the more you squeeze a sponge, the more you get. But others are like a honeycomb—which just overflows with its own sweetness. That is how God gives to us, and it is how we should give in turn.[2]

3. Always be thinking of ways you can give to others in need.

Get creative. Ask yourself, "How can I be the instrument through which someone's needs are met?" Involve others in getting their opinions on how to give to those in need.

4. Realize that the motive for giving is to glorify God, not to get something in return.

The only real motive for giving is so that God may be praised in the process. It reflects upon our God when we live a life of giving. Expect nothing in return for your giving.

5. Make your financial giving biblical.

What is biblical giving? It is consistently giving to God through a local church. The beginning point of biblical giving is the tithe, at least 10 percent of your income. An offering is considered money given above the tithe.

6. Be generous with compliments and praise.

It is within your power to affirm anyone. Someone suggested that we should always be on the lookout for someone doing something right and then compliment him or her. That's a far cry from always trying to find someone doing something wrong.

7. Sacrifice some time for great causes that help people.

Volunteerism is important, but it is also on the decline. Find at least one community-helping program and volunteer some time. It is important that we give of ourselves and not just write a check.

GIVING GIFTS WITH BOTH HANDS

In the Korean culture people give their gifts with both hands. They do this to communicate an important aspect of giving, "I'm not holding anything back. I'm giving you all I have to offer." Such a philosophy should permeate all of our giving whether it is to God or others. Ironically, children are often taught to fold their hands together when praying. With the Korean perspective in mind, this small gesture could be a constant reminder of our commitment to give God all that we have while holding nothing back.[3]

8. Give your forgiveness.

Forgiveness is a sacrificial act of giving. You are sacrificing how you feel because you have been hurt. Forgiveness is surrendering your right to hurt back.

9. Give everything you have to the Lord.

Transfer ownership to the Lord. This is the great exchange. Your money, your home, your car, your things are to be turned over to God. When he is seen as the owner, these will take on a new perspective.

> For it is in giving that we receive.
> —Francis of Assisi

10. Live with "another world" view.

What you give now is sent on to heaven. As you give here on earth, you are moving to heaven before you even get there (see Matt. 6:20). We should live today recognizing we are investing in eternity.

THE HABIT OF
KINDNESS

POINT PASSAGE

When Jesus went ashore, He saw a large crowd, and He felt compassion for them because they were like sheep without a shepherd; and He began to teach them many things.

Mark 6:34

The Jesus habit of kindness is choosing to be sensitive, understanding, gentle, and compassionate to everyone you meet.

> Let us be kind to one another for most of us are fighting a hard battle.
>
> —Dan Maclaren

Jesus Showed Us How to Be Kind

Jesus was kind, sensitive, understanding, and compassionate. He was never hateful, rude, difficult, or untactful. That kindness, however, became firmness in some situations. Kindness is not allowing people to use and abuse us. Jesus' habit of kindness was often directed toward those who couldn't do anything for him.

Jesus was kind to people in need.

And Jesus called His disciples to Him, and said, "I feel compassion for the people, because they have remained with Me now three days and have nothing to eat; and I do not want to send them away hungry, for they might faint on the way." (Matt. 15:32)

Jesus noticed and expressed kindness to all people. It didn't matter who it was, Jesus showed kindness. Christian kindness must have no age, gender, socioeconomic, political, or religious boundaries.

Jesus' kindness moved him to do something about people's problems.

Moved with compassion, Jesus touched their eyes; and immediately they regained their sight and followed Him. (Matt. 20:34)

When Jesus went ashore, He saw a large crowd, and He felt compassion for them because they were like sheep without a shepherd; and He began to teach them many things. (Mark 6:34)

Jesus did something. His compassion was feeling pain in his heart followed by action to alleviate the need.

Jesus was kind to those who had experienced a loss.

When the Lord saw her, He felt compassion for her, and said to her, "Do not weep." (Luke 7:13)

A mother was devastated by the loss of her son. Jesus stopped the funeral and brought him back to life.

SENSELESS KINDNESS

We are repulsed by the all-too-familiar phrase, "random acts of senseless violence." It occurs daily in the newspapers and on TV. Chuck Wall, professor of human relations at Bakersfield College in California, was repulsed enough to do something about it. He assigned his students to "do something out of the ordinary to help someone who isn't expecting it, then write about it." The essays included stories about a student who bought thirty blankets for the homeless and a woman who reparked her car one-half mile from her destination so a frantic-looking motorist could park in her spot near the door. Bumper stickers were made and sold by the students to benefit the Kern County Braille Center. They read, "Today, I will commit one random act of senseless kindness, will you?" Professor Wall stumbled upon a new twist on an old message: "Let us consider how to stimulate one another to love and good deeds" (Heb. 10:24).[1]

All around us are people who have experienced a loss—loss of money, job, marriage, a loved-one to death, health, or faith. Kindness can become a healing agent. It's amazing how a little kindness can bring someone out of discouragement.

> **A kind word never broke anyone's mouth.**
> **—Irish Proverb**

Jesus was kind even to people who let him down

So when they had finished breakfast, Jesus said to Simon Peter, "Simon, son of John, do you love Me more than these?" He said to Him, "Yes, Lord; You know that I love You." He said to him, "Tend My lambs." He said to him again a second time, "Simon, son of John, do you love Me?" He said to Him, "Yes, Lord; You know that I love You." He said to him, "Shepherd My sheep." He said to him the third time, "Simon, son of John, do you love Me?" Peter was grieved because He said to him the third time, "Do you love Me?" And he said to Him, "Lord, You know all things; You know that I love You." Jesus said to him, "Tend My sheep.

"Truly, truly, I say to you, when you were younger, you used to gird yourself and walk wherever you wished; but when you grow old, you will stretch out your hands and someone else will gird you, and bring you where you do not wish to go." Now this He said, signifying by what kind of death he would glorify God. And when He had spoken this, He said to him, "Follow Me!"

Peter, turning around, saw the disciple whom Jesus loved following them; the one who also had leaned back on His bosom at the supper and said, "Lord, who is the one who betrays You?" So Peter seeing him said to Jesus, "Lord, and what about this man?" Jesus said to him, "If I want him to remain until I come, what is that to you? You follow Me!" Therefore this saying went out among the brethren that that disciple would not die; yet Jesus did not say to him that he would not die, but only, "If I want him to remain until I come, what is that to you?"

This is the disciple who is testifying to these things and wrote these things, and we know that his testimony is true.

And there are also many other things which Jesus did, which if they were written in detail, I suppose that even the world itself would not contain the books that would be written. (John 21:15–25)

Peter is a great example of someone who let Jesus down. He denied him, yet Jesus demonstrated kindness to him.

> **Kindness: Love in action.**
> —**Charles Allen**[2]

Jesus was kind to those who were ungrateful.

While He was on the way to Jerusalem, He was passing between Samaria and Galilee. As He entered a village, ten leprous men who stood at a distance met Him; and they raised their voices, saying, "Jesus, Master, have mercy on us!" When He saw them, He said to them, "Go and show yourselves to the priests." And as they were going, they were cleansed. Now one of them, when he saw that he had been healed, turned back, glorifying God with a loud voice, and he fell on his face at His feet, giving thanks to Him. And he was a

---

Don't Shoot the Wounded!

A couple of rednecks are out in the woods hunting when one of them suddenly grabs his chest and falls to the ground. He doesn't seem to be breathing; his eyes are rolled back in his head. The other guy whips out his cell phone and calls 9I!. He gasps to the operator, "I think Bubba is dead! What should I do?" The operator, in a calm soothing voice says, "Just take it easy and follow my instructions. First, let's make sure he's dead." There is a silence, and then a shot is heard. The guy's voice comes back on the line, "OK, now what?" Sometimes it seems we Christians are the only ones who shoot our wounded instead of restoring those who are overtaken in a fault.[3]

Samaritan. Then Jesus answered and said, "Were there not ten cleansed? But the nine—where are they? Was no one found who returned to give glory to God, except this foreigner?" And He said to him, "Stand up and go; your faith has made you well." (Luke 17:11–19)

Jesus healed ten lepers, yet only one came back and thanked Him.

Jesus was kind to sinners

Although kind to all sinners, he always shared the truth with them. We see it with the woman at the well (see John 4:7–8). Yet we see his kindness to sinners in the woman caught in adultery.

> Constant kindness can accomplish much. As the sun makes ice melt, kindness causes misunderstanding, mistrust, and hostility to evaporate.
> —Albert Schweitzer

The scribes and the Pharisees brought a woman caught in adultery, and having set her in the center of the court, they said to Him, "Teacher, this woman has been caught in adultery, in the very act. Now in the Law Moses commanded us to stone such women; what then do You say?" They were saying this, testing Him, so that they might have grounds for accusing Him. But Jesus stooped down and with His finger wrote on the ground. But when they persisted in asking Him, He straightened up, and said to them, "He who is without sin among you, let him be the first to throw a stone at her." (John 8:3–7)

The thief on the cross, the rich young ruler, and Nicodemus were all sinners who received Jesus' kindness.

What Are the Enemies of the Habit of Kindness?

1. Self-centeredness—Why do I have to be kind? No one worries about being kind to me.
2. Lack of concern—I've got my own problems.
3. Bitterness—Where has being kind got me?

4. Busyness—I'm too busy to take my time to do something for someone else.

SOMEONE IS ALWAYS WATCHING

A woman pulls up to a red light behind one other car. She notices the driver of the car in front of her is talking on his cell phone and appears to be shuffling through some papers on the seat beside him. The light turns green, but the man doesn't notice the light change. The woman begins pounding on her steering wheel and yelling at the man to move! The man doesn't move! The woman is going ballistic inside her car, ranting and raving at the man, pounding on her steering wheel and dash. The light turns yellow. The woman begins to blow the car horn, then rolls down her window and begins screaming curses at the man. The man, hearing the commotion, looks up, sees the yellow light, and accelerates through the intersection just as the light turns red. The woman is beside herself, screaming and frustrated, as she misses her chance to get through the intersection. As she is still in mid-rant she hears a tap on her window and looks up into the barrel of a gun held by a serious looking policeman. The policeman tells her to shut off her car while keeping both hands in sight. She complies and is speechless at what is happening.

After she shuts off the engine, the policeman orders her to exit the car with her hands up. The woman gets out of the car, and the policeman orders her to turn and place her hands on the car. She turns, places her hands on the car roof, and quickly is cuffed and hustled into the patrol car. The woman is too bewildered by the chain of events to ask any questions, and she is driven to the police station—where she is fingerprinted, photographed, searched, booked, and placed in a cell.

After a couple of hours, a policeman approaches the cell and opens the door for her. She is escorted back to the booking desk where the original officer is waiting with her personal effects The policeman hands her the bag containing her things and says, "I'm sorry for this mistake, but you see, I pulled up behind your car while you were blowing your horn and cussing a blue streak at the car in front of you. I noticed the 'Jesus loves all of us' license plate holder, and the 'Follow me to Sunday school' bumper sticker, and the chrome plated Christian fish emblem on the trunk, so naturally I assumed you had stolen the car!"

Make Kindness a Habit

1. Determine to be kind to everyone you meet.

Kindness is a mind-set that can be developed. Without discrimination, choose to be kind to every person. Make it your daily assignment.

2. Understand that people are either going into a storm, in a storm, or just coming out of a storm. Everybody's having a hard time.

Give people the benefit of the doubt. Pray for those who don't receive your kindness. Again, you never know what people are going through. Don't take it personally.

3. Smile. It encourages people.

Anyone can smile. A smile is contagious. It gives people a momentary lift and helps change the attitude not only of the one who sees the smile but also of the one who gives it.

4. Do a kind act for someone at least once a week.

Find ways to do specific kind things for someone. Make a list of people you will target for your random acts of kindness.

5. Write an encouraging note to people in your past who have made a difference in your life.

It will help you and encourage them. A kind word to someone may make all the difference in his or her life. We owe a debt of kindness due to the kindness God has shown to us.

6. Take the initiative to speak to people.

Don't wait for people to speak to you. Go first. Even if you are shy, you can learn to do this. Once you begin to take the initiative, it gets easier.

7. Take the time to stop and listen to people who are hurting.

Kindness takes the time to care, to inquire, to hear what's going on in a person's life. Simply stopping and paying attention to someone can be the greatest act of kindness toward that person.

8. Never be kind expecting anything in return.

The joy is in the act of kindness, not the accolade for it. To expect something in return for your kindness is to lose the blessing that comes with the kindness. Kindness is about giving, not getting.

9. Befriend someone the world has abandoned.

They are everywhere—people the world has overlooked, neglected, or abandoned. Your kindness toward that person may be the catalyst to turn his life around. There is power in kindness to break the curse of neglect.

10. If you have been unkind, go back and apologize.

We can all think of those moments when we have been unkind to someone. Swallow your pride and approach that person and humbly say, "Please forgive me." Let the person know that the Jesus who lives inside of you would not tolerate that in your life.

> **Kind words can be short and easy to speak, but their echoes are truly endless.**
> —**Mother Teresa**

THE HABIT OF
FITNESS

POINT PASSAGE

*And Jesus kept increasing in wisdom and stature,
and in favor with God and men.*
LUKE 2:52

The Jesus habit of fitness is choosing to take care of your body through a combination of a healthy diet and regular exercise.

Jesus Showed Us How to Be Fit

Jesus was physically fit. He took care of His body.

And Jesus kept increasing in wisdom and stature, and in favor with God and men. (Luke 2:52)

The word *stature* means he grew physically as a child. It is from his lifestyle, however, that we gain the greatest insight into his physical condition.

In a study from the Mayo Clinic on the life of Jesus prior to his beatings and crucifixion, they share the following: "The rigors of Jesus' ministry (that is, traveling by foot throughout Palestine) would have precluded any

Physical fitness is not only one of the most important keys to a healthy body; it is the basis for dynamic and creative intellectual activity. The relationship between the soundness of the body and the activities of the mind is subtle and complex. Much is not yet understood. But we do know what the Greeks knew: that intelligence and skill can only function at the peak of their capacity when the body is healthy and strong; that hardy spirits and tough minds usually inhabit sound bodies.
—John F. Kennedy

major physical illness or a weak general constitution. Accordingly, it is reasonable to assume that Jesus was in good physical condition before his walk to Gethsemane."[1]

Jesus was God, but he was God in the flesh, God in a body. To be able to accomplish all the Father desired for him, he would have had to have taken care of his body.

What Are the Enemies of the Habit of Fitness?

1. Schedule—Not enough time.
2. Lethargy—I'm too tired.
3. Excuses—I'm not athletic.
4. Procrastination—I will one of these days.

JESUS WALKED ALMOST THE DISTANCE AROUND THE WORLD!

Grand total of miles Jesus walked in his thirty-three years on earth while traveling on trips:
- 400 miles—Jesus walked from Egypt to Nazareth
- 18,000 miles—Jesus walked from Nazareth to Jerusalem and return by age 30
- 3,125 miles—Jesus walked during his three-year public ministry.

Grand total miles Jesus walked on trips—21,525 miles. An average of 20 miles a day on all His journeys would mean that Jesus spent at least 1,076 days and nights on the road in his life! This is a total of two years, 346 days on the road in his life! All these miles he walked by the age of thirty-three. The distance around the world at the equator is 24,901.55 miles. This means the Jesus walked almost the distance around the world! Looking at the above mileage Jesus walked and knowing that he traveled much more than listed, I personally believe he walked the distance around the world that he had made with the Father and the Holy Spirit. "In the beginning was the Word, and the Word was with God, and the Word was God. He was in the beginning with God. All things were made through Him and without Him nothing was made that was made. In Him was life, and the life was the light of men!" (John 1:1–4).[2]

Make Fitness a Habit

1. Make a commitment to the Lord to do the best you can to take care of your body.

It is your responsibility to maintain your body so that it works as the Creator intended for it to work. Do all you can do to ensure a healthy body. Ask God to help you with this every day.

2. Realize that your body is not your own as a Christian. It belongs to Jesus Christ.

You give up your rights to do with your body what you want to do with it. That means everything you do with your body needs to reflect God's ownership. We are managers of God's property.

3. Find your ideal weight and start now on a journey toward it.

That can be a painful experience, but it is necessary. You need to know the goal weight for which you need to be striving. It won't happen overnight, but this is a great place to begin. Now you have a goal, a written-down goal.

4. Schedule exercise at least three times a week.

It could be walking, running, swimming, or anything cardio-vascular. Consistency is the key. You will not see results without discipline. Start somewhere and start now.

5. Begin now by watching your diet.

Be sensible. Read about foods that are good for your heart. Limit the fast food you take into your body.

STRENUOUS EXERCISE LEADS TO POSITIVE ATTITUDE CHANGE

A study, which put sixty middle-aged men through a strenuous exercise program, resulted in positive attitude change. "The personality scores of the men who were in the worst condition to begin with, showed the greatest level of improvement. . . . Scores went up on personality tests that measured emotional stability, imagination, self-assurance, and self-sufficiency."[3]

6. Have a fitness accountability partner.

That has been the strength of groups like Weight Watchers. Whether with a group or simply with another person, have someone to whom you are accountable. Give the other person permission to ask you the hard questions about your fitness.

7. Avoid fad diets.

Make eating right a lifestyle, rather than looking for weight management in quick fixes. Quick fixes may work immediately, but they are not a long-term solution. Fitness must become a way of life, not a short-term, lose-weight mind-set. If not, the weight will come back since no overall lifestyle changes were made.

8. Don't believe the too-good-to-be-true advertisements.

They don't work. You will not lose ten pounds in three days. You will not get fit without sacrifice. There is no easy way to get fit, and anyone who claims so is simply attempting to sell some

---

PHYSICAL HEALTH
A NATURAL OUTCOME

Few biblical texts specifically delineate the benefits and perhaps requirements for physical fitness. Perhaps this is because physical health was a natural outcome of lifestyle in Jesus' day. Transportation systems consisted of little more than walking or riding an animal. Jesus' disciples were fishermen, and his own trade was carpentry. Who felled the trees needed for Jesus' handiwork? How were the nets, bulging with fish, hauled back into the boat? The work demanded by these tasks was entirely manual.[4]

TAKE CARE OF YOURSELF

Mickey Mantle never expected to live beyond the age of forty. His father and grandfather both died by forty. Unfortunately, Mantle abused his body with alcohol for forty-three years. Upon reflection at age sixty-two, Mantle said, "If I'd known I was going to live this long, I'd have taken better care of myself." Now is a great time to start taking bet-

program. We have heard it before: if it seems too good to be true, it is.

9. Don't become overly preoccupied with your body.

The body must not take priority over the soul. As important as the body is, to become obsessed with the body is to place one's attention on that which is not eternal. The body is aging and will eventually die. However, one's soul lives forever.

10. Make your body the best it can be, but accept the body style that God has given to you.

It's difficult to do, but stop comparing your body with others. Don't have unrealistic expectations because of what you see in a magazine, on a billboard, or on television. Accept the body God has given to you, then work to make it all God intended.

A DIETER'S PRAYER

Lord, grant me the strength that I may not fall
Into the clutches of cholesterol.
At polyunsaturates, I'll never mutter,
For the road to hell is paved with butter.
And cake is cursed and cream is awful
And Satan is hiding in every waffle.
Beelzebub is a chocolate drop
And Lucifer is a lollipop.
Teach me the evils of hollandaise,
Of pasta and globs of mayonnaise.
And crisp fried chicken from the south—
Lord, if you love me, shut my mouth.[6]

THE HABIT OF
KEEPING
YOUR WORD

POINT PASSAGE

*"But let your statement be, 'Yes, yes' or 'No, no';
anything beyond these is of evil."*
MATTHEW 5:37

The Jesus habit of keeping your word is choosing consistently to do what you say, following through with what you promise.

> Promises may get friends, but it's performance that keeps them.
> —Owen Feltham

Jesus Showed Us How to Keep Our Word

Jesus always did what he said he would do. There is never an instance in Scripture when he said he would do something that he didn't follow through with it. His track record was perfect. What Jesus said and did were one. We call that integrity. Consistency in word and deed was truly one of Jesus' greatest examples. Be encouraged, he is still keeping his Word!

Jesus told the centurion that his servant was healed.

And when Jesus entered Capernaum, a centurion came to Him, imploring Him, and saying, "Lord, my servant is lying paralyzed at home, fearfully tormented." Jesus said to him, "I will come and heal him." . . . And

Jesus said to the centurion, "Go; it shall be done for you as you have believed." And the servant was healed that very moment. (Matt. 8:5–7, 13)

By the time the centurion got home, Jesus had kept his word and the man's servant was healed.

Jesus allowed Mary to pour perfume on him, and he made a statement about the future that he is still keeping

"She has done what she could; she has anointed My body beforehand for the burial. Truly I say to you, wherever the gospel is preached in the whole world, what this woman has done will also be spoken of in memory of her." (Mark 14:8–9)

We are still talking about it today.

KEEPING PROMISES

Writer and speaker Lewis Smedes says: Yes, somewhere people still make and keep promises. They choose not to quit when the going gets rough because they promised once to see it through. They stick to lost causes. They hold on to a love grown cold. They stay with people who have become pains in the neck. They still dare to make promises and care enough to keep the promises they make. I want to say to you that if you have a ship you will not desert, if you have people you will not forsake, if you have causes you will not abandon, then you are like God.

What a marvelous thing a promise is! When a person makes a promise, she reaches out into an unpredictable future and makes one thing predictable: she will be there even when being there costs her more than she wants to pay. When a person makes a promise, he stretches himself out into circumstances that no one can control and controls at least one thing: he will be there no matter what the circumstances turn out to be. With one simple work of promise, a person creates an island of certainty in a sea of uncertainty.

When a person makes a promise, she stakes a claim on her personal freedom and power. When you make a promise, you take a hand in creating your own future."[1]

Jesus told Martha that Lazarus would live again.

Jesus said to her, "I am the resurrection and the life; he who believes in Me will live even if he dies, and everyone who lives and believes in Me will never die. Do you believe this?" . . .

Jesus said, "Remove the stone." Martha, the sister of the deceased, said to Him, "Lord, by this time there will be a stench, for he has been dead four days." Jesus said to her, "Did I not say to you that if you believe, you will see the glory of God?" So they removed the stone. Then Jesus raised His eyes, and said, "Father, I thank You that You have heard Me. I knew that You always hear Me; but because of the people standing around I said it, so that they may believe that You sent Me." When He had said these things, He cried out with a loud voice, "Lazarus, come forth." The man who had died came forth, bound hand and foot with wrappings, and his face was wrapped around with a cloth. Jesus said to them, "Unbind him, and let him go." (John 11:25–26, 39–44)

Jesus brought Lazarus back to life from the grave.

Jesus announced that he was the resurrection.

Jesus answered them, "Destroy this temple, and in three days I will raise it up." . . . So when He was raised from the dead, His disciples remembered that He said this; and they believed the Scripture and the word which Jesus had spoken. (John 2:19, 22)

Jesus said to her, "I am the resurrection and the life; he who believes in Me will live even if he dies." (John 11:25)

"He is not here, for He has risen, just as He said. Come, see the place where He was lying." (Matt. 28:6)

Jesus kept his word; he rose from the dead.

What Are the Enemies of the Habit of Keeping Your Word?

1. Procrastination—When I get around to it, I will.
2. Selfishness—When I made that commitment, I wasn't busy.
3. Convenience—I didn't realize what I was getting myself into. It's too much trouble.
4. Circumstances—Things have changed.

Make Keeping Your Word a Habit

1. Remember what you tell people you will do for them.

Write it down. Don't depend on your memory. You can easily forget it. Follow through with what you say as soon as possible.

Samuel Goldwyn said, "A verbal agreement isn't worth the paper it's written on." No promise, verbal or written, is of any value except in relation to the integrity of the one who makes the promise. Some recall a time when "a man's word was his bond." If we make promises, we ought to keep them. God does.
—Robert C. Shannon[2]

2. If you promise something, even if your circumstances change, keep your promise.

Your integrity is on the line, and so is Christ's reputation. Your word is obligatory regardless of the things that come up after you gave your word.

3. Apologize if you have not kept your word.

Don't make excuses. Don't try to justify it. Admit you messed up and seek the person's forgiveness. Determine you will never again put yourself in that position.

4. If you aren't sure you can do it, don't promise it.

It is better to say no and then do it than to say yes and then not do it. Count the cost first. Know what you are getting yourself into. Ask specific questions. Once you have all the information you need, then give your answer. If you need time to think and pray about it, tell the person; just make sure you are not using that as a cop-out or stalling technique.

5. Don't tell one person one thing and another person something else.

That inconsistency will eventually come to light; it always does; when it does it will damage your credibility. You gain the reputation of someone who cannot be trusted. No trust, no impact for God.

6. Work diligently to make sure your words and actions are consistent.

Jesus had much to say about this. He called it hypocrisy. Nothing hurts one's reputation like saying one thing and doing another. Perhaps this has done more damage to the gospel than any other enemy.

7. When you give your word, ask God to give you the strength to keep it.

Commit it to God immediately and ask for his power to follow through and do what you said. He will give you whatever strength you need to keep your word. Trust him.

MICHAEL JORDAN KEEPS HIS WORD

In his book *Lessons from a Father to His Sons,* Senator John Ashcroft writes: "Until 1997, Michael Jordan, indisputably the leading player in the NBA for over a decade, was never the highest paid player. When asked why he did not do what so many other players do—hold out on their contracts until they get more money—Michael replied, 'I have always honored my word. I went for security. I had six-year contracts, and I always honored them. People said I was underpaid, but when I signed on the dotted line, I gave my word.'"

Three years later, after several highly visible players reneged on their contracts, a reporter asked Michael once again about being underpaid, and he explained that if his kids saw their dad breaking a promise, how could he continue training them to keep their word? By not asking for a contract renegotiation, Michael Jordan spoke volumes to his children. He told them, "You stand by your word, even when that might go against you." His silence became a roar.[3]

8. Don't say yes too quickly just to get people off your back at the moment.

It may sound good at the moment, but weigh the consequences before you say, "Sure," "OK," "Why not," or "I'll do it." This is often an attempt to make yourself look good, but the time will come when you are expected to keep your word.

9. Remember, keeping your word defines your character.

You will be judged by the way you do what you say. You are known by how you keep your word. Jesus will be judged by how you follow through with your promises.

10. Above all, keep your word to God.

When you tell God you will do something, do it! Breaking your word to God is a serious matter. If you have failed to keep your word to God, confess it immediately to him and get back on track.

THE HABIT OF
FELLOWSHIPPING

POINT PASSAGE

*Jesus, therefore, six days before the Passover, came to Bethany
where Lazarus was, whom Jesus had raised from the dead.
So they made Him a supper there, and Martha was serving;
but Lazarus was one of those reclining at the table with Him.
Mary then took a pound of very costly perfume of pure nard,
and anointed the feet of Jesus and wiped His feet with her hair;
and the house was filled with the fragrance of the perfume.*
JOHN 12:1–3

The Jesus habit of fellowshipping is
choosing to spend time with other
Christians on a regular basis for the
purpose of enjoyment.

> Christians are not
> lone rangers.
> —Chuck Colson

*Jesus Showed Us
How to Fellowship*

Jesus enjoyed being with people. Often we see him enjoying
the company of friends and family. He felt comfortable eating in
their homes. Even when he was a guest, Jesus became the host,
serving others. Christians need times of being together sharing
their common bond in Christ.

Jesus enjoyed being with people.

Then it happened that as Jesus was reclining at the
table in the house, behold, many tax collectors and

sinners came and were dining with Jesus and His disciples. (Matt. 9:10)

He said, "Yes." And when he came into the house, Jesus spoke to him first, saying, "What do you think, Simon? From whom do the kings of the earth collect customs or poll-tax, from their sons or from strangers?" (Matt. 17:25)

And immediately after they came out of the synagogue, they came into the house of Simon and Andrew, with James and John. (Mark 1:29)

> **The Bible knows nothing of a solitary religion.**
> —John Wesley

While He was in Bethany at the home of Simon the leper, and reclining at the table, there came a woman with an alabaster vial of very costly perfume of pure nard; and she broke the vial and poured it over His head. (Mark 14:3)

When Jesus came to the place, He looked up and said to him, "Zaccheus, hurry and come down, for today I must stay at your house." (Luke 19:5)

Jesus loved to be in the homes of people enjoying their company.

Jesus enjoyed eating with people.

While they were eating, Jesus took some bread, and after a blessing, He broke it and gave it to the disciples, and said, "Take, eat; this is My body." (Matt. 26:26)

Twice Jesus held a food-fest.

After these things Jesus went away to the other side of the Sea of Galilee (or Tiberias). A large crowd followed Him, because they saw the signs which He was performing on those who were sick. Then Jesus went up on the mountain, and there He sat down with His disciples. Now the Passover, the feast of the Jews, was near. Therefore Jesus, lifting up His eyes and seeing that a large crowd was coming to Him, said to

Philip, "Where are we to buy bread, so that these may eat?" This He was saying to test him, for He Himself knew what He was intending to do. Philip answered Him, "Two hundred denarii worth of bread is not sufficient for them, for everyone to receive a little." One of

BLEST BE
THE TIE THAT BINDS

John Fawcett was converted as a teenager listening to George Whitefield. He joined the Baptists and was ordained on July 31, 1765. He began pastoring a poor church in Wainsgate, finding time here and there for writing. His writings spread abroad, and the little church feared they would lose their pastor to a larger place. Fawcett wondered the same thing, lamenting in his diary that his family was growing faster than his income. The call came from London's famous Carter's Lane Church. "Think of it!" Fawcett told his wife. "They want us in London to take the place of the late Dr. Gill at that great church! It's almost unbelievable!" The following Sunday he broke the news to his church, then began packing. Books, dishes, pictures, and furniture were crated for the overland journey to the world's largest city. When the day of departure came, church members assembled and bravely tried to hold their tears. Finally everything was loaded but one box, and

Fawcett entered the house to retrieve it. There he found his wife deep in thought. "John," she said, voice breaking, "do you think we're doing the right thing? Will we ever find a congregation to love us and help us with the Lord's work like this group here?" "Do you think we've been too hasty in this?" John asked. "Yes. I think we should stay right here and serve these people." John was silent a moment, for his heart, too, had been breaking. He nodded, "I was so overjoyed when the call came that I never really prayed about it like a minister should." They walked onto the porch, called the people together, revealed their change of heart, and amid joyous tears unloaded their wagons. Fawcett stayed at Wainsgate the rest of his life. But not in obscurity. Out of this experience, he wrote the world-famous hymn:

> Blest be the tie that bind
> Our hearts in Christian love.
> The fellowship of kindred minds
> Is like to that above.[1]

His disciples, Andrew, Simon Peter's brother, said to Him, "There is a lad here who has five barley loaves and two fish, but what are these for so many people?" Jesus said, "Have the people sit down." Now there was much grass in the place. So the men sat down, in number about five thousand. Jesus then took the loaves, and having given thanks, He distributed to those who were seated; likewise also of the fish as much as they wanted. When they were filled, He said to His disciples, "Gather up the leftover fragments so that nothing will be lost." So they gathered them up, and filled twelve baskets with fragments from the five barley loaves which were left over by those who had eaten. (John 6:1–13)

And Jesus called His disciples to Him, and said, "I feel compassion for the people, because they have remained with Me now three days and have nothing to eat; and I do not want to send them away hungry, for they might faint on the way." The disciples said to Him, "Where would we get so many loaves in this desolate place to satisfy such a large crowd?" And Jesus said to them, "How many loaves do you have?" And they said, "Seven, and a few small fish." And He directed the people to sit down on the ground; and He took the seven loaves and the fish; and giving thanks, He broke them and started giving them to the disciples, and the disciples gave them to the people. And they all ate and were satisfied, and they picked up what was left over of the broken pieces, seven large baskets full. And those who ate were four thousand men, besides women and children.

And sending away the crowds, Jesus got into the boat and came to the region of Magadan. (Matt. 15:32–39)

Often you see Jesus using food as a point of fellowship. There's something about sharing a meal that builds community.

Jesus celebrated with fellowship after his resurrection.

> Jesus said to them, "Come and have breakfast." None of the disciples ventured to question Him, "Who are You?" knowing that it was the Lord. Jesus came and took the bread and gave it to them, and the fish likewise. This is now the third time that Jesus was manifested to the disciples, after He was raised from the dead. (John 21:12–14)

After his resurrection he desired to fellowship with those to whom he was closest.

What Are Enemies of the Habit of Fellowshipping?

1. Busyness—I just don't have the time.
2. Unforgiveness—I don't want to be around people.
3. Broken relationships—I don't trust people.
4. Jealousy—They have more than me.

> You need to be in fellowship of a church. . . . If you separate a live coal from the others, it will soon die out. However, if you put a live coal in with the other live coals, it will be a glow that will last for hours.
> —**Billy Graham, from** *World Aflame*

Make Fellowshipping a Habit

1. Realize that you are related to every Christian on the planet.

Every Christian has a common Father. We are interrelated with one another. We make up the body of Christ. That's the reason we can meet someone for the first time in a place far away and feel we already know the person. It is because of our connectedness in Christ.

2. Acknowledge that you need other people.

Pride often keeps us from admitting what we know on the inside. We need other people. No Christian should attempt to be a Lone Ranger—attempting to live without the encouragement and help of others.

3. Get together with other Christians at least once a week.

This is not a luxury; it is a necessity that Christians on a regular basis come together for fellowship. There are a variety of ways that could happen each week such as Sunday school, small groups, or in-home fellowships.

4. Develop the great art of being a good listener.

One of the ingredients of successful fellowship is the art of paying attention to people and genuinely caring enough to listen to them. Listening fosters great fellowship.

5. Share a meal with others at least once a month.

Get together in someone's home. Go out together for a relaxing meal. Great conversation can occur over a meal. It provides an opportunity to get to know people. We tend to drop our guards in that kind of setting allowing people to see a glimpse of the real us.

6. Encourage your children to have friends in your home.

Make your home children friendly, teenage friendly. Open your home to your children's friends. You will be doing yourself and them a favor.

7. Ask God to bring people into your life with whom you are compatible.

God will honor your prayer as you sincerely seek him in this matter. Trust him to bring divine appointments into your life. Be on the lookout; the answer could come from unexpected places or people.

8. Be consistent in attending the church where you belong. If you don't belong to one, find one.

You will make some of your best friends at church. It is the greatest place to build lasting relationships. Belonging to a church, not just attending one, is vital to fellowship.

> "You know, the only thing I miss is the fellowship I used to have with all the guys down at the tavern. We used to sit around, laugh, and drink a pitcher of beer, tell stories, and let our hair down. I can't find fellowship like that with Christians."
> —A recently converted Christian[2]

9. Choose to forgive those who have wronged you in the church.

Let it go. Life is too short to hold a grudge. Don't judge the whole church because one or even a few have let you down or hurt you. Be a person that offers a second chance.

10. Be wise in selecting the people with whom you will spend the most time.

"Do not be deceived: Bad company corrupts good morals." (1 Cor. 15:33) You become like the people with whom you spend the most time. As your friends go, so go you. Seek out fellowship with God-centered, scriptural-principled people.

THE HABIT OF
USING
SCRIPTURE

POINT PASSAGE

But Jesus answered and said to them, "You are mistaken, not understanding the Scriptures nor the power of God."
MATTHEW 22:29

The Jesus habit of using Scripture is choosing consistently to study and apply God's Word to everyday life situations, whether temptations, trials, or triumphs.

> **Back to the Bible or back to the Jungle.**
> —Luis Palau

Jesus Showed Us How to Use Scripture

Jesus knew the Old Testament Scriptures. He used them to guide his life. Jesus knew Scripture so well that when something was misquoted, misused, taken out of context, counterfeited, added to, or taken away, he could immediately spot it. That should be the goal of every Christian.

George Barna, in his book *Think Like Jesus,* said:

Personally, the most convincing argument is that Jesus Christ taught that the Bible is God's authoritative words to humankind. By personally endorsing the value and veracity of the Scriptures, Jesus empowers us to be totally confident that the Bible is reliable and authoritative. How does Jesus endorse the Bible? In His teaching He frequently quoted passages of the Old Testament or based His lessons upon stories contained in those books. When He argued with religious leaders and teachers, His tendency was to draw them back to Scripture and rely upon the authority of the Word—and the result was that they resented being shown up but could neither contradict the wisdom nor challenge the source.[1]

Jesus used Scripture to engage Satan in spiritual warfare.

During the wilderness temptations by Satan, Jesus used Scripture to defeat him and gain spiritual victory. He quoted Deuteronomy 8:3; 6:16; 6:13; 10:20.

> But He answered and said, "It is written, 'Man shall not live on bread alone, but on every word that proceeds out of the mouth of God.'" Jesus said to him, "On the other hand, it is written, 'You shall not put the Lord your God to the test.'"

AN UNFAIR CONTEST

A Christian university student shared a room with a Muslim. As they became friends, their conversation turned to their beliefs. The believer asked the Muslim if he'd ever read the Bible. He answered no, but then asked if the Christian had ever read the Koran. The believer responded, "No, I haven't, but I'm sure it would be interesting. Why don't we read both together, once a week, alternating books?" The young man accepted the challenge, their friendship deepened, and during the second term he became a believer in Jesus. One evening, late in the term, he burst into the room and shouted at the longtime believer, "You deceived me!" "What are you talking about?" the believer asked. The new believer opened his Bible and said, "I've been reading it through, like you told me, and just read that the Word is living and active!" He grinned, "You knew all along that the Bible contained God's power and that the Koran is a book like any other. I never had a chance!" "And now you'll hate me for life?" queried the believer. "No," he answered, "but it was an unfair contest."[2]

Then Jesus said to him, "Go, Satan! For it is written, 'You shall worship the Lord your God, and serve Him only.'"

Then the devil left Him; and behold, angels came and began to minister to Him. (Matt. 4:4, 7, 10–11)

Victories are won through applying Scripture.

Jesus believed in the authority of Scripture

"But Abraham said, 'They have Moses and the Prophets; let them hear them.' But he said, 'No, Father Abraham, but if someone goes to them from the dead, they will repent!' But he said to them, 'If they do not listen to Moses and the Prophets, neither will they be persuaded if someone rises from the dead.'" (Luke 16:29–31)

"For if you believed Moses, you would believe Me, for he wrote about Me. But if you do not believe his writings, how will you believe My words?" (John 5:46–47)

Jesus believed every word of the Hebrew Scriptures and counted them as the final authority on any subject. He knew the power of God's Word.

Jesus used Scripture to point out doctrinal error

But Jesus answered and said to them, "You are mistaken, not understanding the Scriptures nor the power of God." (Matt. 22:29)

Jesus pointed out the error of the Sadducees by using Scripture.

Jesus used Scripture to teach people the truth

And He said to them, "O foolish men and slow of heart to believe in all that the prophets have spoken! Was it not necessary for the Christ to suffer these things and to enter into His glory?" Then beginning with

Moses and with all the prophets, He explained to them the things concerning Himself in all the Scriptures.

And they approached the village where they were going, and He acted as though He were going farther. But they urged Him, saying, "Stay with us, for it is getting toward evening, and the day is now nearly over." So He went in to stay with them. When He had reclined at the table with them, He took the bread

B.I.B.L.E.—Basic Instructions Before Leaving Earth —Unknown

and blessed it, and breaking it, He began giving it to them. Then their eyes were opened and they recognized Him; and He vanished from their sight. They said to one another, "Were not our hearts burning within us while He was speaking to us on the road, while He was explaining the Scriptures to us?" And they got up that very hour and returned to Jerusalem, and found gathered together the eleven and those who were with them, saying, "The Lord has really risen and has appeared to Simon." They began to relate their experiences on the road and how He was recognized by them in the breaking of the bread.

While they were telling these things, He Himself stood in their midst and said to them, "Peace be with you." But they were startled and frightened and thought that they were seeing a spirit. And He said to them, "Why are you troubled, and why do doubts arise in your hearts? See My hands and My feet, that it is I Myself; touch Me and see, for a spirit does not have flesh and bones as you see that I have." And when He had said this, He showed them His hands and His feet. While they still could not believe it because of their joy and amazement, He said to them, "Have you anything here to eat?" They gave Him a piece of a broiled fish; and He took it and ate it before them.

Now He said to them, "These are My words which I spoke to you while I was still with you, that all things which are written about Me in the Law of Moses and the Prophets and the Psalms must be fulfilled." Then He opened their minds to understand the Scriptures, and He said to them, "Thus it is written, that the Christ would suffer and rise again from the dead the third day." (Luke 24:25–46)

Jesus showed the disciples from Emmaus, returning from the crucifixion and now back home, how the Law, the prophets, and the Psalms had equal authority. He further used Scripture to make application to himself. He revealed Scripture to show people the truth.

Jesus used Scripture to show of his coming resurrection.

Then some of the scribes and Pharisees said to Him, "Teacher, we want to see a sign from You." But He answered and said to them, "An evil and adulterous generation craves for a sign; and yet no sign will be given to it but the sign of Jonah the prophet; for just as Jonah was three days and three nights in the belly of the sea monster, so will the Son of Man be three days and three nights in the heart of the earth. The men of Nineveh will stand up with this generation at the judgment, and will condemn it because they repented at the preaching of Jonah; and behold, something greater than Jonah is here." (Matt. 12:38–41)

MTV JOURNALIST
ON BIBLE READING

MTV political correspondent Tabitha Soren says: "No matter how secular our culture becomes, it will remain drenched in the Bible. Since we will be haunted by the Bible even if we don't know it, doesn't it make sense to read it?"[3]

Jesus pointed back to Jonah to show of his coming resurrection.

Jesus used Scripture to make sense of what was happening in his arrest, trial, and crucifixion.

"The Son of Man is to go, just as it is written of Him; but woe to that man by whom the Son of Man is betrayed! It would have been good for that man if he had not been born." And Judas, who was betraying Him, said, "Surely it is not I, Rabbi?" Jesus said to him, "You have said it yourself."

> **The Bible does not mean merely to inform but to transform.**
> **—Unknown**

While they were eating, Jesus took some bread, and after a blessing, He broke it and gave it to the disciples, and said, "Take, eat; this is My body." And when He had taken a cup and given thanks, He gave it to them, saying, "Drink from it, all of you; for this is My blood of the covenant, which is poured out for many for forgiveness of sins. But I say to you, I will not drink of this fruit of the vine from now on until that day when I drink it new with you in My Father's kingdom."

After singing a hymn, they went out to the Mount of Olives.

Then Jesus said to them, "You will all fall away because of Me this night, for it is written, 'I will strike down the shepherd, and the sheep of the flock shall be scattered.' But after I have been raised, I will go ahead of you to Galilee."

While He was still speaking, behold, Judas, one of the twelve, came up accompanied by a large crowd with swords and clubs, who came from the chief priests and elders of the people. Now he who was betraying Him gave them a sign, saying, "Whomever I kiss, He is the one; seize Him." Immediately Judas went to Jesus and said, "Hail, Rabbi!" and kissed Him. And Jesus said to him, "Friend, do what you have come for." Then they came and laid hands on Jesus and seized Him.

And behold, one of those who were with Jesus reached and drew out his sword, and struck the slave of the high priest and cut off his ear. Then Jesus said to him, "Put your sword back into its place; for all those who take up the sword shall perish by the sword. Or do you think that I cannot appeal to My Father, and He will at once put at My disposal more than twelve legions of angels? How then will the Scriptures be fulfilled, which say that it must happen this way?" (Matt. 26:24–32, 47–54)

> No one ever graduates from Bible study until he meets the Author face-to-face.
> —Everett Harris

When Jesus had spoken these words, He went forth with His disciples over the ravine of the Kidron, where there was a garden, in which He entered with His disciples. Now Judas also, who was betraying Him, knew the place, for Jesus had often met there with His disciples. Judas then, having received the Roman cohort and officers from the chief priests and the Pharisees, came there with lanterns and torches and weapons. So Jesus, knowing all the things that were coming upon Him, went forth and said to them, "Whom do you seek?" They answered Him, "Jesus the Nazarene." He said to them, "I am He." And Judas also, who was betraying Him, was standing with them. So when He said to them, "I am He," they drew back and fell to the ground. Therefore He again asked them, "Whom do you seek?" And they said, "Jesus the Nazarene." Jesus answered, "I told you that I am He; so if you seek Me, let these go their way," to fulfill the word which He spoke, "Of those whom You have given Me I lost not one." Simon Peter then, having a sword, drew it and struck the high priest's slave, and cut off his right ear; and the slave's name was Malchus. So Jesus said to Peter, "Put the sword into the sheath; the cup which the Father has given Me, shall I not drink it?" (John 18:1–11)

Scripture helps us to make sense out of what is happening in our lives.

What Are the Enemies of the Habit of Using Scripture?

1. Ignorance—I don't know what the Bible says.
2. Busyness—I don't have time to read the Bible.
3. Lack of exposure—I'm not going to church or a Bible study right now.
4. Indifference—What can an antiquated book teach me about my life in the twenty-first century?

Make Using Scripture a Habit

1. Read the Bible every day. Have a specific plan of reading.

Don't wait until you sit down with an open Bible to decide what you will read. Know beforehand and then get right to it. Several great Bible-reading plans are available, many of which you can pull right off of the Internet.

2. Commit to reading the Bible through every year.

Use a different translation each year. The One-Year Bible is a helpful tool.

Every Christian should read the Bible through at least once. This adds credibility to one's faith.

BIBLE QUOTING
COMPETITION MURDER

Not long ago a Bible quoting competition in a southern US city ended in the murder of one of the two finalists. After the two had argued over the wording of a verse of Scripture, one rushed home, picked up a gun, returned, and shot the other.[4]

3. Expose yourself to the Bible being taught at least once a week.

Seek a knowledgeable Bible instructor for weekly group instruction. It is vital to our spiritual health that we are spiritually fed from God's Word. God has gifted certain people to teach the Bible. Each time we expose ourselves to biblical preaching and teaching, we have the opportunity to grow spiritually.

4. Use the Bible to determine if something is doctrinally correct. Ask for the chapter and verse.

Don't accept it just because someone says, "God said it," or "God told me." Always go back to the Bible. If it is not consistent with the Bible, drop it like a hot potato.

5. Use biblical principles to determine moral issues.

Although there may not be a specific verse relating to a matter, God's Word is filled with principles on which we can decide right and wrong. Any issue a Christian faces can be answered by using scriptural principles.

6. Use Scripture to comfort you when you are sorrowful or facing a loss.

The book of Psalms is one of the greatest sources of encouragement ever penned. Nothing brings comfort and assurance like a word from God. Whatever you are facing, there is a comforting passage that will speak directly to your need.

7. Use Scripture to judge experience; don't use your experience to judge Scripture.

Our experiences are not the authority by which we judge truth or error. We begin with an open Bible. If our experience is not consistent with Scripture, then there is something vitally wrong with our experience. A true experience with God always conforms to the Bible.

8. Keep a copy of the Bible with you—in your car, home, office.

Always have it handy. You will be amazed at how often during the day, if you have a Bible, you will open it and read it. Always be ready for God to say something to you through his Word.

9. Memorize Scripture.

There is power in hiding God's Word in your mind and heart. It benefits you no matter what you are facing, whether a temptation or a moment of worry. To be able to recall a specific portion of the Bible becomes a great defense against Satan's fiery darts of doubt.

10. Apply Scripture.

Scripture becomes powerful within your life at the point of application. It is the doing of the Word that brings true happiness. To know God's Word brings you knowledge, but to do God's Word brings you life's greatest moments.

THE HABIT OF
PURPOSE

POINT PASSAGE

*"For the Son of Man has come to seek and
to save that which was lost."*

Luke 19:10

The Jesus habit of purpose is choosing to have your reason for living as serving God and making a difference for him in the world.

> More men fail through lack of purpose than through lack of talent.
> —Billy Sunday

Jesus Showed Us His Purpose

Jesus ordered his schedule, his daily routine, through his purpose. Everything he did was ordered by his purpose. Every person he healed, sermon he preached, miracle he performed, word he spoke, and prayer he prayed was so people could be saved.

The beatings, the cross, the resurrection, and the ascension were all about his purpose of winning the lost.

Why do you get out of bed in the morning? What drives you? What are you passionate about? Where are you going with your life?

Jesus had the purpose of bringing people into the kingdom of God.

"But go and learn what this means: 'I desire compassion, and not sacrifice,' for I did not come to call the righteous, but sinners." (Matt. 9:13)

"For the Son of Man has come to seek and to save that which was lost." (Luke 19:10)

"For I have come down from heaven, not to do My own will, but the will of Him who sent Me. This is the will of Him who sent Me, that of all that He has given Me I lose nothing, but raise it up on the last day. For this is the will of My Father, that everyone who beholds the Son and believes in Him will have eternal life, and I Myself will raise him up on the last day." (John 6:38–40)

> **I want to take our entire culture and push it closer to God.**
> **—Phil Vischer, creator of Veggie Tales®**

That was the central purpose of his life, to save the lost. That must become the purpose of every Christian, to share the life-changing message of the gospel.

Jesus came to fulfill the law and the prophets.

Do not think that I came to abolish the Law or the Prophets; I did not come to abolish but to fulfill. (Matt. 5:17)

Jesus was the One who would complete every law and every prophecy. He accomplished his purpose.

THE FUEL OF HAPPINESS

British theologian C. S. Lewis described happiness fifty years ago in terms that make even more sense today in our commuter-driven society: "A car is made to run on gasoline, and it would not run properly on anything else. Now God designed the human machine to run on himself. He himself is the fuel our spirits were designed to burn, or the food our spirits were designed to feed on. There is no other. That is why it is just no good asking God to make us happy in our own way without bothering about religion. God cannot give us a happiness and peace apart from himself, because it is not there. There is no such thing."[1]

Jesus came to serve.

"For even the Son of Man did not come to be served, but to serve, and to give His life a ransom for many." (Mark 10:45)

Jesus was the epitome of a servant. He exemplified this attitude in all he did.

Jesus came to bring life beyond what anyone had ever experienced.

"The thief comes only to steal and kill and destroy; I came that they may have life, and have it abundantly." (John 10:10)

> Every life should have a purpose to which it can give the energies of its mind and the enthusiasms of its heart. That life without a purpose will be prey to the perverted ways waiting for the uncommitted life.
> —C. Neil Strait

Jesus not only came to bring eternal life but abundant life here on earth. He came not only to take us to heaven when we die but also to give us a life worth living now.

Jesus came to be a light to the world.

Jesus therefore said to them, "For a little while longer the light is among you. Walk while you have the light, that darkness may not overtake you; he who walks in the darkness does not know where he goes. While you have the light, believe in the light, in order that you may become sons of God. (John 12:35–36)

In a spiritually dark world, Jesus came to shine the light on the need for a Savior. Further he showed the overcoming that could take place when the Savior is received.

Jesus came to tell us the truth about God and us.

Therefore Pilate said to Him, "So You are a king?" Jesus answered, "You say correctly that I am a king. For this I have been born, and for this I have come into the world, to testify to the truth. Everyone who is of the truth hears My voice." (John 18:37)

Jesus showed us that truth will always lead us to God.

Jesus came to destroy the devil's work.

The one who practices sin is of the devil; for the devil has sinned from the beginning. The Son of God appeared for this purpose, to destroy the works of the devil. (1 John 3:8)

Jesus fulfilled Scripture.

"And I will put enmity between you and the woman, and between your seed and her seed; he shall bruise you on the head, and you shall bruise him on the heel." (Gen. 3:15)

He destroyed what the devil had set out to accomplish, to make death an enemy that couldn't be destroyed.

> The purpose of your life is far greater than your own personal fulfillment, your peace of mind, or even your happiness. It's far greater than your family, your career, or even your wildest dreams and ambitions. If you want to know why you were placed on this planet, you must begin with God. You were born by his purpose and for his purpose.
> —Rick Warren[2]

What Are the Enemies of the Habit of Purpose?

1. Comfort—It would take me out of my comfort zone.
2. Apathy—I'm satisfied with the way things are.
3. Laziness—I'm too tired to take on one more thing.
4. Ignorance—I don't know why I'm here or what God wants me to do.

Make Purpose a Habit

1. Realize that God has a specific plan for your life.

Just think, the same God who created the world has a unique purpose for you. God has a design for every human being. You are significant to God. You play a role for him on planet Earth.

2. Discover that God's purpose for your life is a process.

The process is the most important part of the journey. God's will is unfolded one step at a time. He doesn't reveal the whole plan at once. If he did, faith would be unnecessary.

3. Ask God to show you his purpose for your life.

Prayer is a vital part of discovering God's purpose. Through prayer God gives us insight and wisdom into his will. Prayer creates the climate where God's purposes can be more clearly seen.

4. Live your life to please God and serve him.

The core value of your life must be that in everything you do, God is pleased and honored. This should be the filter through which you make every decision.

A CHANCE TO CHANGE THE WORLD!

Steve Jobs is a whiz at making computers, but there was a time when he needed some help in marketing his incredible little "magic boxes." He was in need of an expert who could help him take his Apple Computers into the ring against IBM. John Sculley became the target of Steve Jobs' attention. Sculley, at age thirty-eight, had been Pepsi-Cola's youngest president. He masterminded the Pepsi Generation ad campaign that dethroned Coke from the number one position for the first time in history. Steve Jobs knew it would take a lot to get Sculley. He wined and dined him and made numerous offers with money he didn't even have, all to no avail. Sculley was content with his present and secure success. Finally, in desperation, Steve Jobs threw out a question of exasperation, *"Do you want to spend the rest of your life selling sugared water, or do you want a chance to change the world?"* It was that single, piercing question which leveraged the greatest weight in John Sculley's decision to leave his security at Pepsi and go to Apple for an opportunity to "change the world." Christians, more than computers, have the "real" opportunity to change the world. Let's not miss our purpose by remaining content simply to sell "sugared water."[3]

5. Prioritize what is important to God.

Schedule your priorities. God says that he is to be first, followed by your marriage partner, your children, then your job. It is imperative that what is most important to God is most important to you.

> "God has something only you can do."
> —Lewis Timberlake

6. Your purpose can best be demonstrated in your daily routine, not in some big event.

Stop looking for the big event and realize that God's purpose shows up most often in your daily schedule. You never know in a routine day how God will break in and reveal his specific purpose for you. That makes the Christian life exciting everyday.

7. Make sure you spend your time on the eternally significant.

The only two things in life that are eternal are the Bible and people. Give your life to promoting the Bible and investing in people. Don't play Trivial Pursuit with the life God has given you.

8. Get up every day knowing what you say and do can matter for God.

You can make a difference for God. Your contribution can be vital to the kingdom. God has given you an assigned seat in life. Use that seat, your influence right where you are, for him.

9. Understand that there is more to life than what you can see, hear, taste, or smell. There is a spiritual dimension.

It is within that dimension you will experience your greatest fulfillment. When the spiritual dimension is put first, it will affect every other area of our lives.

10. Live to leave a legacy, something life altering that you leave behind.

What you do while you are living can continue after you are gone. Give your life to that which will outlive you and impact people for Christ for years to come.

THE HABIT OF
FASTING

*And after He had fasted forty days and
forty nights, He then became hungry.*
MATTHEW 4:2

The Jesus habit of fasting is choosing to
go without food for a specific time in
order to seek God and his will with
more passion and intensity.

> Fasting without prayer
> is starvation.
> —Unknown

Jesus Showed Us How to Fast

Jesus knew firsthand the power of fasting. When he fasted,
supernatural things happened. Jesus fasted for forty days and forty
nights. Supernatural things happen for us too when we fast
according to God's Word. Fasting can change your life.

Jesus was confronted by Satan with the most vicious and
intense attacks possible.

Jesus fasted to overcome Satan.

Then Jesus was led up by the Spirit into the wilderness to be tempted by the devil. And after He had fasted
forty days and forty nights, He then became hungry.
And the tempter came and said to Him, "If You are the
Son of God, command that these stones become bread."
But He answered and said, "It is written, 'Man shall not
live on bread alone, but on every word that proceeds
out of the mouth of God.'"

Then the devil took Him into the holy city and had Him stand on the pinnacle of the temple, and said to Him, "If You are the Son of God, throw Yourself down; for it is written, 'He will command His angels concerning You'; and 'On their hands they will bear You up, so that You will not strike Your foot against a stone.'" Jesus said to him, "On the other hand, it is written, 'You shall not put the Lord your God to the test.'"

> Jesus spent time alone with God, seeking solitude to hear the voice of His Father in heaven. He fasted in order to remind Himself to focus on God. —George Barna[1]

Again, the devil took Him to a very high mountain and showed Him all the kingdoms of the world and their glory; and he said to Him, "All these things I will give You, if You fall down and worship me." Then Jesus said to him, "Go, Satan! For it is written, 'You shall worship the Lord your God, and serve Him only.'" Then the devil left Him; and behold, angels came and began to minister to Him. (Matt. 4:1–11)

As Long as It Takes

Pastor Stephen Bly, of Winchester, Idaho, was fortunate to have witnessed the beauty of discipleship in one of his church members. August Jensen was an eighty-four-year-old widower who sat toward the back in church. Many perceived him as one who no longer had much to offer. His pastor learned otherwise. On a visit to Gus's house, Pastor Bly saw the old man's daily regimen. He spent two and a half hours in Bible study and prayer followed by a three-mile walk where he conversed with God. Lately he had been fasting two meals a day and praying for the salvation of Anthony, a neighborhood teen who was good for little more than mischief. The pastor asked, "How long have you been fasting and praying for him like that?" Gus replied, "Forty days." "How much longer will you continue?" wondered his pastor. With a smile, Gus said, "As long as it takes." On day fifty-one, Anthony committed his life to Christ.[2]

Fasting helped him to face Satan's temptations. It gave him the strength to deflect Satan's darts. He could more clearly see God's plan for his life. Fasting helped him to get through the crisis.

Jesus assumed Christians would fast.

"Whenever you fast, do not put on a gloomy face as the hypocrites do, for they neglect their appearance so that they will be noticed by men when they are fasting. Truly I say to you, they have their reward in full." (Matt. 6:16)

Jesus said *when you fast* not *if you fast*. He wanted us to follow his example.

Jesus taught the true way to fast.

"Whenever you fast, do not put on a gloomy face as the hypocrites do, for they neglect their appearance so that they will be noticed by men when they are fasting. Truly I say to you, they have their reward in full. But you, when you fast, anoint your head and wash your face so that your fasting will not be noticed by men, but by your Father who is in secret; and your Father who sees what is done in secret will reward you." (Matt. 6:16–18) Jesus gives us the plan for effective fasting.

> Prayer is reaching out after the unseen; fasting is letting go of all that is seen and temporal. Fasting helps express, deepen, confirm the resolution that we are ready to sacrifice anything, even ourselves to attain what we seek for the kingdom of God.
> —Andrew Murray

What Are the Enemies of the Habit of Fasting?

1. Inconvenience—It would affect my schedule too much.
2. Comfort—I don't like feeling hungry.
3. Unwillingness—I just don't want to do that.

Make Fasting a Habit

1. Let God lead you as to when you fast.

Follow the burden the Lord places upon your heart as to when and how you fast. This is not to suggest that having a regular time each week to fast is wrong; however, one should always be sensitive to those times God specifically calls him to fast.

2. Fast for something specific.

Make a list. This will become your prayer target throughout your time of fasting. You need to have certain things in mind so you will know when God has answered them.

3. Fasting and prayer always go together.

You can pray without fasting, but fasting should never be done apart from prayer. Fasting helps us to focus our praying. It creates an atmosphere where intense prayer can take place.

4. Fast to express your availability to God.

Fasting is your way of saying, "God, I am available to hear from you and to do anything you tell me to do." It sets you apart as one who is waiting for God's orders so you can say yes.

5. Fast to put your body under the Lord's control.

Fasting helps us to discipline our bodies. Our bodies have the tendency to dictate to us what we will do. It is a way to place the physical part of us in a position of submission to God.

TYPES OF FASTING

Supernatural Fast

Fasting for many days without food and water. Seeing that the average human can only last about three days without water, this type of fast needs supernatural strength. Therefore, you must be sure that God is definitely leading you to undertake this type of fast. Undertaken by Moses (Deut. 9:9–18; Exod. 34:28), and Elijah (1 Kings 19:8).

Absolute Fast

Where no water or food is taken (this should only be done for short periods of time—maximum three days (Esther 4:16; Acts 9:9).

Normal Fast

This is when no food is taken but water/liquids are taken during the fast. The Bible shows that this can be undertaken for one to forty days (some people in history have fasted for longer) (Matt. 4:1–2).

Partial Fast

Abstention from certain types of food (Dan. 1:8; 10:3, Num. 6:3). Possibly undertaken by John the Baptist (Matt. 3:4).

Public/National/Church Fast

When a body of people cooperatively join together in a fast for a specific purpose (Esther 4:3; Jon. 3:6; Acts 13:1–3).[3]

6. Don't tell anyone, with the exception of your spouse, you are fasting.

Jesus taught us not to go around announcing the fact that we are fasting. Fasting is never to call attention to us. Quite the opposite, it is to take the spotlight off of us and onto listening to the Lord.

> Fasting is a divine corrective to the pride of the human heart. It is a discipline of body with a tendency to humble the soul.
> —Arthur Wallis

7. Reserve enough time to spend alone with God during your fast.

It is vital that time be built in during the fast in order to seek God. The time we would normally use to eat should instead be used to pray. Don't allow that time to be filled with other busy stuff.

8. Don't get discouraged if you do not see an immediate answer.

Sometimes you may see immediate answers or sense an immediate relief. However, most of the time it is a process of seeing God move in answer to prayer and fasting. We must always trust God's timing and leave the results of our fasting up to him.

> If the reward you aim at in fasting is the admiration of others, that is what you will get, and that will be all you get. In other words, the danger of hypocrisy is that it is so successful. It aims at the praise of men, and it succeeds. But that's all.
> —John Piper[4]

9. Make sure you are fasting for the right reasons.

It is not to lose weight. That is never to be the motive. However, if one consistently practices the discipline of fasting, it does benefit weight management. The only motive for fasting should be to seek God and glorify him through the answer.

10. Be joyful because you have done something tangible for God by denying yourself.

Fasting is something measurable. You can look back at this time and know that you acted upon a biblical discipline. When you fast, you have identified with Jesus Christ and his many disciples who practiced fasting.

THE HABIT OF
USING MONEY
GOD'S WAY

POINT PASSAGE

"For where your treasure is, there your heart will be also."
MATTHEW 6:21

The Jesus habit of using money God's way is using your money to support the kingdom of God, meeting your needs and those of your family, and saving for the future.

Jesus Showed Us How to Use Money God's Way

He demonstrated how God expects each of us to handle money and possessions. Jesus understood the blessings and dangers of money.

Jesus paid what he owed.

> When they came to Capernaum, those who collected the two-drachma tax came to Peter and said, "Does your teacher not pay the two-drachma tax?" He said, "Yes." And when he came into the house, Jesus spoke to him first, saying, "What do you think, Simon? From

Fifteen percent of everything Christ said relates to this topic (money and possessions)—more than His teachings on heaven and hell combined. Why did Jesus put such an emphasis on money and possessions? Because there's a fundamental connection between our spiritual lives and how we think about and handle money. We may try to divorce our faith and our finances, but God sees them as inseparable.
—Randy Alcorn[1]

whom do the kings of the earth collect customs or poll-tax, from their sons or from strangers?" When Peter said, "From strangers," Jesus said to him, "Then the sons are exempt. However, so that we do not offend them, go to the sea and throw in a hook, and take the first fish that comes up; and when you open its mouth, you will find a shekel. Take that and give it to them for you and Me."

> We make a living by what we get. We make a life by what we give.
> —Winston Churchill[2]

"Show Me the coin used for the poll-tax." And they brought Him a denarius. And He said to them, "Whose likeness and inscription is this?" They said to Him, "Caesar's." Then He said to them, "Then render to Caesar the things that are Caesar's; and to God the things that are God's." And hearing this, they were amazed, and leaving Him, they went away. (Matt. 17:24–27; 22:19–22)

Jesus was committed to paying what he owed. He understood his earthly obligations and met every one of them. He paid his taxes.

Jesus understood the dangers of money

"Do not store up for yourselves treasures on earth, where moth and rust destroy, and where thieves break in and steal. But store up for yourselves treasures in heaven, where neither moth nor rust destroys, and where thieves do not break in or steal; for where your

---

RICHARD PRYOR CALLS ON GOD

Comedian Richard Pryor was critically burned in an accident in 1980. Appearing later on the *Johnny Carson Show,* he insisted that when you are seriously ill, money isn't important: "All that I could think of was to call on God. I didn't call the Bank of America once."[3]

treasure is, there your heart will be also. . . . No one can serve two masters; for either he will hate the one and love the other, or he will be devoted to one and despise the other. You cannot serve God and wealth." (Matt. 6:19–21, 24)

Looking at him, Jesus felt a love for him and said to him, "One thing you lack: go and sell all you possess and give to the poor, and you will have treasure in heaven; and come, follow Me." (Mark 10:21)

Then He said to them, "Beware, and be on your guard against every form of greed; for not even when one has an abundance does his life consist of his possessions." (Luke 12:15)

HAPPINESS AT THE GOLDEN ARCHES

When we take our children to the shrine of the Golden Arches, they always lust for the meal that comes with a cheap little prize, a combination christened, in a moment of marketing genius, the Happy Meal. You're not just buying fries, McNuggets, and a dinosaur stamp; you're buying happiness. Their advertisements have convinced my children they have a little McDonald's-shaped vacuum in their souls: "Our hearts are restless till they find their rest in a Happy Meal." I try to buy off the kids sometimes. I tell them to order only the food, and I'll give them a quarter to buy a little toy on their own. But the cry goes up, "I want a Happy Meal." All over the restaurant, people crane their necks to look at the tight-fisted, penny-pinching cheapskate of a parent who would deny a child the meal of great joy. The problem with the Happy Meal is that the happy wears off, and they need a new fix. No child discovers lasting happiness in just one: "Remember that Happy Meal? What great joy I found there!" Happy Meals bring happiness only to McDonald's. You ever wonder why Ronald McDonald wears that grin? Twenty billion Happy Meals, that's why. When you get older, you don't get any smarter; your Happy Meals just get more expensive.[4]

Jesus warned us not to put our trust in money, but instead he showed us to put our trust in God and invest in eternity by using money for kingdom purposes. He knew that wherever we invest our money, our heart, focus, and passion would follow.

With the rich young ruler he demonstrated that money and things can easily be put ahead of God and could cost someone his soul. It is not a sin to be rich; it is sinful when money is placed ahead of God.

Jesus showed that when you put God first, every need will be met.

"But seek first His kingdom and His righteousness, and all these things will be added to you." (Matt. 6:33)

> Each of us will eventually give away all our earthly possessions. How we choose to do so, however, is a reflection of our commitment to the kingdom of God.
> —Charles Stanley

"And do not seek what you will eat and what you will drink, and do not keep worrying. For all these things the nations of the world eagerly seek; but your Father knows that you need these things. But seek His kingdom, and these things will be added to you. . . . For where your treasure is, there your heart will be also." (Luke 12:29–31, 34)

Jesus showed us that when God is first, every need in our bodies will be met—that's every need, not every greed. It is our job to

---

MONEY WILL BUY . . .

. . . a bed, but not sleep.	. . . amusements, but not happiness.
. . . books, but not brains.	
. . . food, but not appetite.	. . . a crucifix, but not a Savior.
. . . finery, but not beauty.	. . . religion, but not salvation.
. . . a house, but not a home.	. . . a good life, but not eternal life.
. . . medicine, but not health.	
. . . luxuries, but not culture.	. . . a passport to everywhere but heaven.[5]

obey; it is God's job to keep his Word, and he always keeps his Word.

Jesus showed us that no one can outgive God.

"Give, and it will be given to you. They will pour into your lap a good measure—pressed down, shaken together, and running over. For by your standard of measure it will be measured to you in return." (Luke 6:38)

Jesus knew that when we obey God and have faith in him he will bless us far beyond what we have given. God delights in blessing his obedient children.

What Are the Enemies to the Habit of Using Money God's Way?

1. Selfishness—It's my money, I earned it, it's all mine.
2. Greed—I want to use my money for what I want. Why should I give to someone else? No one has ever done anything for me.
3. Worry—I'm afraid if I give to God I can't pay my bills.
4. Indebtedness—I want to use my money God's way, but I'm too far in debt.

THE ADMIRAL SPEAKS

Basketball star David Robinson, "The Admiral," feeds the homeless through his Feed My Sheep program, and he helps needy families get diapers and baby food through a charity called The Ruth Project. Here's what he says about such giving: "These aren't sacrifices for me. If I'm clutching on to my money with both hands, how can I be free to hug my wife and kids?"[6]

Make Using Money God's Way a Habit

1. Transfer ownership of your money and possessions over to God.

By an act of your will, tell God that everything you have is now being turned over to him. You are now a manager of God's resources, formerly known as "mine."

2. You cannot outgive God but have fun trying.

God will meet every need of our lives when we put him first. God delights in meeting our needs when we obey him in the area of finances. Scripture is filled with promises of multiple blessings to those who give God's way.

> There is nothing at all wrong with having money unless money has you.
>
> —Norman Vincent Peale

3. Remember, your giving to God is a matter of faith and obedience, not about money per se.

God doesn't need our money. He can do just fine without it. However, he does desire our faith and obedience in order to accomplish his purpose in and through us. Money is often the instrument through which faith and obedience are demonstrated.

4. Ask yourself on a regular basis, "Have I put my money and things ahead of God?"

Remember Jesus' warnings of how easily money can take the top spot in our lives. That will be a constant struggle. Take inventory and ask yourself the hard question of, "Has money become more important than God and my family?"

5. Be generous; refuse to be greedy.

Miser is the root word for *miserable*. Generous people are happy people. Jesus told us, "It is more blessed to give than receive." (Acts 20:35) Don't keep a tight grip on anything material.

6. Tithing, giving 10 percent of your income to God, is the minimum basis for biblical giving.

Jesus affirmed tithing.

> "Woe to you, scribes and Pharisees, hypocrites! For you tithe mint and dill and cummin, and have neglected the weightier provisions of the law: justice and mercy

and faithfulness; but these are the things you should have done without neglecting the others." (Matt. 23:23)

Tithing preceded the Old Testament Law. Grace giving involves tithing and beyond. Settle the tithing issue, and great peace and blessings will follow.

> Money is in some respects like fire; it is a very excellent servant, but a terrible master.
> —P. T. Barnum

7. Develop a savings plan now.

Have as a goal saving 10 percent of your check. Start somewhere and work toward that goal. Planning for the future is a scriptural principle.

8. Give offerings above your tithe to support other ministries.

Find kingdom-impacting ministries you can financially support. Make sure the organization is biblically based and has high accountability in the handling of finances.

9. Be passionately committed to paying your debts on time.

Christians should be impeccable in their reputation for paying their bills. Our credibility and Christ's is often tied to the way we consistently handle the debts we owe.

10. Keep in mind, some things are more important than money.

These are things money cannot buy, such as a relationship with God, friends, a good reputation, and health. Prioritize that which money cannot purchase.

ENDNOTES

Introduction

1. Napoleon Bonaparte, cited in *The Book of Jesus,* edited by Calvin Miller (New York: Touchstone, 1996, 1998), 63–64.

2. Raymond McHenry. *McHenry's Stories for the Soul* (Peabody, Mass.: Hendrickson Publishers, 2001), 138.

3. "I Am a Habit," anonymous quote.

4. George Barna, *Think Like Jesus* (Brentwood, Tenn.: Integrity, 2003), 14.

1. The Habit of Seclusion

1. Daniel DeNoon, "Songs Stick in Everyone's Head," 27 February 2003, *WebMD Medical News,* 1–2.

2. *Management Digest,* July 1989; www.christianglobe.com.

2. The Habit of Prayer

1. The Presidential Prayer Team, www.presidentialprayerteam.org?id=9.

3. The Habit of Worship

1. Darren Ethier, *The New Lexicon:Webster's Encyclopedic Dictionary of the English Language* (Ottawa: Lexicon, 1988), 1135.

2. Neil MacQueen, "Too Good to Be True—The Life Benefits of Regular Church Attendance," www.sundaysoftware.com/stats.htm.

3. Thomas Rainer, *Surprising Insights from the Unchurched and Proven Ways to Reach Them* (Grand Rapids, Mich.: Zondervan, 2001), 33.

4. George Barna, *Grow Your Church from the Inside Out* (Ventura, Calif.: Regal Books, 2002), 32.

5. Neill MacQueen, *Too Good to Be True: The Life Benefits of Regular Church Attendance,* quoted from Barna Research Group, www.barna.org.

6. Ibid.

7. Amber Johnson, "Want Better Grades? Go to Church," *Christianity Today,* 21 May 2002, 60.

4. Habit of Building Relationships

1. Fred Sigle, Evangelism, www.sermoncentral.com.

2. Dale Carnegie, *How to Win Friends and Influence People* (New York: Simon and Schuster, 1936), 58.

3. Quote from *Baptist Program,* August 1991, 23.

4. Quote by Ron Parrish, sermon, Hope Chapel, Austin, Texas, 19 November, 1994.

5. John Mark Ministries, quoting Bryan G. Dyson, Georgia Tech's 1972 Commencement, 6 September 1991, www.pastor.net.au/jmm/articles/9992.htm.

5. The Habit of Touch

1. Kathleen Keating, *The Hug Therapy Book* (Minneapolis, Minn.: Compcare Publishers, 1983), 11–14.

2. Alan Smith, www.dailly-blessings.cm/bless419.htm.

3. Bob Brigham, The Man Who Invented the High Five, quoted in *The Diamond Angle.*

6. The Habit of Confrontation

1. Marabel Morgan in *Homeside,* February 1987, quoted in www.sermonillustrations.com, www.christianglobe.cvom/illustrations/the details.asp?whichone=c&whichfile=confrontation.

7. The Habit of Challenging the Status Quo

1. Jay Livingston and Ray Evans, "Que Sera Sera" song written for Alfred Hitchcock's 1956 remake of his 1934 film *The Man Who Knew Too Much,* starring Doris Day and James Stewart. Recorded by Doris Day.

2. Ed Rowell, from *The Tennessean,* 12 September 1999.

3. Robert D. Dale, *To Dream Again* (Nashville: Broadman, 1981), 20.

4. Mark Eppler, *The Wright Way* (New York: AMACOM, 2004), 95, 107.

8. The Habit of Listening

1 "Hearing God, Preaching Today, www.biblecener.com/illustrations/hearinggod.htm.

2. Raymond McHenry, *McHenry's Quotes, Quotes, and Other Notes* (Peabody, Mass.: Hendrickson Publishers, 1998), 49.

3. www.wow4u.com/communication.

9. The Habit of Love

1. Craig Brian Larson, ed., "The Graham's Unexpected Hospitality," *Perfect Illustrations* (Wheaton, Ill.: Tyndale House Publishers, 2002), 182–83.

2. James Botts, "Love," www.sermoncentral.com.

3. Dave Barry, "Birds Suddenly Appear," *The Story File,* 199, from *Book of Bad Songs* (Kansas City, Mo.: Andrews McMeel Publishing, 2000).

10. The Habit of Thankfulness

1. www.Cybersalt.org.

2. Roy B. Zuck, *The Speaker's Quote Book* (Grand Rapids, Mich.: Kregel, 1997), 381.

3. "Thankfulness," www.sermoncentral.com, contributed by Troy Mason.

11. The Habit of Faith

1. www.Christianglobe.com/illustrations, April 2004.

2. Craig Brian Larson, ed., "The Giver's Big Hands," *More Perfect Illustrations* (Wheaton, Ill.: Tyndale House, 2003), 305.

3. Ibid., "Praying in Faith," 96.

12. The Habit of Motivation

1. Craig Brian Larson, ed., "Motivation," *More Perfect Illustrations* (Wheaton, Ill.: Tyndale House, 2003), 188.

2. Roy Zuck, *The Speakers' Quote Book* (Grand Rapids, Mich.: Kregel, 1997), 265.

3. Raymond McHenry, *McHenry's Stories for the Soul* (Peabody, Mass.: Hendrickson Publishers, 2001), 47.

13. The Habit of Handling Criticism Effectively

1. Raymond McHenry, *McHenry's Stories for the Soul* (Peabody, Mass.: Hendrickson Publishers, 2001), 60–61.

2. The late T. W. Wilson was Billy Graham's executive assistant.

3. Marshall Shelley, *Well Intentioned Dragons* (Carol Stream, Ill.: Christianity Today, 1988), 61.

14. The Habit of Family Priority

1. www.sumnerwemp.com, April 2004.

2. Craig Brian Larson, interview with James Dobson, "The Family in Crisis," *Focus on the Family,* August 2001, *More Perfect Illustrations* (Wheaton, Ill.: Tyndale House, 2003), 97–98.

3. Quoted by Paul Fritz from Human Development and Family Department at the University of Nebraska-Lincoln, "Family," www.sermoncentral.com.

15. The Habit of Obedience

1. Tom Neven, "A Doer of the Word," *Focus on the Family,* September 2000, in Craig Brian Larson, ed., *More Perfect Illustrations* (Wheaton, Ill.: Tyndale House, 2003).

2. Colin Smith, pastor of Arlington Heights Evangelical Free Church, Arlington Heights, Illinois.

3. Eugene Peterson, *A Long Obedience in the Same Direction* (Downers Grove, IL: InterVarsity Press, 1980), 12.

16. The Habit of Honoring the Government

1. Excerpts from "Vast Majority in U.S. Support 'Under God,'" 30 June 2002. http://www.cnn.com/2002/US/06/29/poll.pledge/index.html.

2. Charles Swindoll, *The Quest for Character* (Grand Rapids, Mich.: Zondervan, 1993), 70.

3. "Our Nation's Godly Heritage," http://www.presidentialprayerteam.org/index_text.htm. 22 August 2002.

4. David R. Lewis, quoting Red Skelton's "Commentary on the Pledge of Allegiance," www.usflag.org/skeltonspledge.html.

5. Michael Savage, *The Savage Nation* (Nashville, Tenn.: WND Books, 2002), 71–72.

17. The Habit of Asking Questions

1. Elisabeth Elliot, *Keep a Quiet Heart* (Ventura, Calif.: Vine Books, 1995).

2. "Silly Lawyers, *Salt Lake Tribune,* www.geocities.com/collegepart/6174/tranqui2.htm.

18. The Habit of Having Fun

1. Roy B. Zuck, *The Speakers Quote Book* (Grand Rapids, Mich.: Kregel Publications, 1997), 221.

2. Bruce Marchiano, *In the Footsteps of Jesus,* www.sermoncentral.com, contributed by Randall Deal.

3. *USA Weekend,* 15 July 1994, 5.

19. The Habit of Truth

1. Hugh Poland, Kingwood, Texas. www.preachingtoday.com/indez.taf.

2. Submitted by Michael W. Owenby, *USA Today,* 28 August 2001.

3. Dr. Perry Buffington, psychologist and author, *"Playing Charades,"* Universal Press Syndicate, 26 September 1999.

20. The Habit of Rest

1. Tim Hansel, *When I Relax I Feel Guilty* (Elgin, Ill.: David C. Cook, 1979), 30.

2. Gary Yates, Roanoke, Virginia; references Martin Moore-Ede, "The Twenty-four Hour Society," *Circadian Information,* 1993.

3. National Sleep Foundation, Sleep Facts and Stats, www.sleepfoundation.org/NSAW/pk-sleepfacts.cfm.

4. Craig Brian Larson, ed., *More Perfect Illustrations* (Wheaton, Ill.: Tyndale House, 2003), 239.

21. The Habit of Acting Like a Man

1. www.seromoncentral.com, contributed by Jeffrey Benjamin.

2. Quote from *Men's Health,* quoted in *Parade Magazine,* 29 December 1991, 5.

3. www.sermoncentral.com, contributed by Davon Huss.

4. Ted Engrstrom, *The Making of a Christian Leader* as quoted in *Charles R. Swindoll, Swindoll's Ultimate Book of Illustrations and Quotes* (Nashville, Tenn.: Thomas Nelson Publishers, 1998), 304–5.

5. "Men vs. Women," www.basicjokes.com/djoke.

22. The Habit of Esteeming Women

1. Helen Foster Snow, "Bound Feet and Straw Sandals," *Woman in Modern China* (Paris: Mouton, 1967).

2. Alvin J. Schmidt, *Under the Influence, How Christianity Transformed Civilization* (Grand Rapids: Zondervan, 2001), 122.

3. "Lack of Courtship Rules Leaves College Women in a Muddle," *Washington Post,* 30 July 2001, submitted by Melissa Parks, Des Plaines, Illinois.

4. www.sermoncentral, contributed by Chad Wright.

5. Ed Young, *Romancing the Home* (Nashville: Broadman & Holman, 1994), 152–54.

23. The Habit of Giving

1. Jack Hyles, Sunday evening sermon, 29 September 1974.

2. Ground Zero, http://www.gzyouth.com/forwards/Quotes.asp

3. Raymond McHenry, *McHenry's Stories for the Soul* (Peabody, Mass.: Hendrickson Publishers, 2001), 121.

24. The Habit of Kindness

1. *Houston Post,* 29 October 1993, A–6.

2. Charles Allen, *The Miracle of Love* (Old Tappan, N.J.: Fleming H. Revell, 1972), 19.

3. "Don't Shoot the Wounded! Kindness," www.summerwemp.com, April 2004.

25. The Habit of Fitness

1. Adapted from Arthur Blessitt, www.arthurblessitt.com/ jesuswalked.html and The-Crucifixion.com, Study on the Physical Death of Jesus Christ, an article from the JAMA by William D. Edwards, MD, Wesley J. Gabel, MDiv., Floyd E. Hosmer, MS, AMI, Health of Jesus, www.frugalsites.net/jesus.

2. Ibid.

3. Kenneth H. Cooper, *The Aerobics Way* (Toronto: Bantam, 1977), 176.

4. *Houston Post,* 29 January 1994, B–2.

5. www.hleewhite.mybravenet.com/Just_Funny/A_Dieters_ Prayer— quoted by Stephen A. Pickert, M.D.

6. Ibid.

26. The Habit of Keeping Your Word

1. Lewis Smedes, *"The Power of Promises,"* A Chorus of Witnesses, edited by Long and Plantinga (Grand Rapids: Eerdmans, 1994).

2. Robert C. Shannon, *1000 Windows* (Cincinnati, Ohio: Standard Publishing, 1997), 200.

3. John Ashcroft, *Lessons from a Father to His Sons* (Nashville: Thomas Nelson, 1998).

27. The Habit of Fellowshipping

1. Robert J. Morgan, "Blest Be the Tie that Binds," *Nelson's Complete Book of Stories, Illustrations and Quotes* (Nashville, Tenn.: Thomas Nelson, 2000), 326–27.

2. Win Arn, Carroll Nyquist, and Charles Arn, *Who Cares About Love?* (Pasadena, Calif.: Church Growth, 1986), 122.

28. The Habit of Using Scripture

1. George Barna, *Think Like Jesus* (Brentwood, Tenn.: Integrity, 2003), 153–54.

2. Floyd Schneider, *Evangelism for the Fainthearted* (Grand Rapids, Mich.: Kregel, 2000); quoted in *Men of Integrity,* March/April 2001.

3. Quote by Tabitha Soren, *USA Weekend,* 13 June 1999.

4. Jim Dyet and Jim Russel, *Overcoming Subtle Sins* (Lansing, Mich.: The Amy Foundation, 2002), 41–42.

29. The Habit of Purpose

1. C. S. Lewis, *Mere Christianity* (New York: Harper Collins, 1952), 50.

2. Rick Warren, *Purpose Driven Life* (Grand Rapids, Mich.: Zondervan, 2002), 17.

3. Raymond McHenry, *McHenry's Quips, Quotes, and Other Notes* (Peabody, Mass.: Hendrickson, 1998), 204–5.

30. The Habit of Fasting

1. George Barna, *Think Like Jesus* (Brentwood, Tenn.: Integrity, 2003), 7.

2. *Moody Monthly,* June 1992, 16.

3. www.wclc.org.uk/sermon/fasting/3.html.

4. John Piper, *A Hunger for God* (Wheaton, Ill.: Crossway Books, 1997), 71.

31. The Habit of Using Money God's Way

1. Randy Alcorn, *The Treasure Principle* (2001), 8.

2. Winston Churchill, quoted in *USA Today,* 10 November 2000, 3B; submitted by Rubel Shelly; Nashville, Tennessee.

3. Peter Graystone, "Ready Salted," *Scripture Union,* 1998, p. 114; submitted by David Holdaway; Stonehaven, Kincardinshire, Scotland.

4. Craig Brian Larson, ed., *Perfect Illustrations* (Wheaton, Ill.: Tyndale House, 2002), 123–24, quoting "Pursuit of Happiness," in John Ortberg, *Dangers, Toils & Snares.*

5. Robert J. Morgan, ed., *Nelson's Complete Book of Stories, Illustrations, & Quotes* (Nashville, Tenn.: Thomas Nelson Publishers, 2000), 575.

6. Adapted from Rick Reilly, "Spur of the Moment," *Sports Illustrated,* 23 June 1999.